THE
Power

OF BEING A
Woman

CHANGING THE WORLD
BY EMBRACING YOUR
FEMININE POWER

THE POWER OF BEING A WOMAN
Changing the World by Embracing Your Feminine Power

Published by:
Empowered Life Productions
www.EmpoweredLifeProductions.com
(954) 543-0434

Book Design by Julie Csizmadia

ISBN: 978-0-9854983-2-0 (paperback)

Self-Help/Women's Studies

THE *Power* OF BEING A *Woman*

CHANGING THE WORLD
BY EMBRACING YOUR FEMININE POWER

WITH
Vanessa Halloum
AND *friends*

Dedication

This book is dedicated to one of strongest women I have ever met, my mother-in-law…

Mrs. Najat Halloum

Table of Contents

CHAPTER 1

Vanessa Halloum

Vanessa Halloum is the author of the multi-award winning book "The 5 Feminine Power Virtues". Her mission is to help spread a message of feminine spirituality, leadership and entrepreneurship and to encourage women to use their voice to ignite positive change in the world.

She's also a holistic marketing coach, speaker and seminar leader. As the president of the Holistic Chamber of Commerce of Greater Fort Lauderdale, she helps mission-driven entrepreneurs attract more of their ideal clients so they can grow their business and make a bigger impact. She spent 15 years working as a marketing executive for Fortune 500 companies managing successful multi-million dollar campaigns. In 2008 she left her Manhattan job to work with conscious entrepreneurs to help them expand their reach, find more clients and increase their impact. She's a certified Business Growth Coach with extensive experience in the areas of marketing strategy and implementation, social media exposure and brand messaging.

Learn more at www.vanessahalloum.com.

My Story and My Journey to Power

I spent most of my adult life climbing the corporate ladder because that's what I was taught to do. My mother wanted me to never depend on a man. She encouraged me to work hard, study hard. I think many of us can relate to those maternal lessons, and I'm grateful for her direction and support. She was (and still is) an amazing teacher and feminine role model.

But as I grew into adulthood and pursued my goals, I realized I was *really* unhappy. I pulled in a substantial salary and climbed the corporate ladder to a VP position at a Fortune 500 company but something felt off, like a square peg in a round hole.

Don't get me wrong: a part of me was proud of my accomplishments, but another part was so unhappy that I would come home and cry for hours. My poor husband didn't know what to do except to ask me what was wrong. He didn't get it. (And frankly neither did I. At least at first.)

Eventually, I left corporate America. It had become too draining and no longer worth it, even with all of the money I was making. It was a hard decision. You get very comfortable with that kind of income. It's hard to give up that lifestyle and start brand new.

I took some time off to do some serious soul-searching. I certainly didn't find all of the answers to life right away, but at least the process was underway. That alone made me feel relieved. And thankfully, the universe eventually provided by offering up exactly the spiritual seminars and retreats I needed for direction. When I finally began to realize that I was living almost completely in a masculine mode, so much opened up for me.

In the corporate world, I had been entrenched in a masculine model that didn't fit me. So of course, I was incredibly unhappy. No one said, "Hey you! You're trying to imitate men and you're *way* off course!"

There are many amazing businesswomen who are powerful and remain true to who they are. But that model was no longer working for me. I needed to return to my true feminine essence in order to get back on track.

Let me clarify something about masculine energy: I don't mean to imply that women should avoid all masculine traits. I wouldn't get work done if I didn't use the masculine aspects inside of me—traits like focus, determination, commitment, and courage.

But there's a difference between leveraging our masculine side and *living* there. Understanding and embracing that difference made a profound change in me. Though it took some time to "rewire" myself, I was determined to make that change.

That's why I wrote my book, *The Five Feminine Power Virtues*. Writing it helped me clarify what I truly believed. You can think about the changes you want to make in your life…but writing about it? That creative process helps solidify your ideas and make them more real. In black and white, in front of you! Writing became part of the healing process, and the principles I detailed in my book truly began to guide my life.

After I finished the book, I knew it was time to share these principles with other women. Having other women join me had to be part of the equation. We could *share* our experiences. Offer guidance. Create a sisterhood. We could foster relationships where we build on the experience of others in order to grow. We could all support each other.

How I Define Power

There are two kinds of power: the state of doing and the state of being. This can also be seen as the masculine and the feminine. Neither one is stronger nor more important. Both need the other in order to exist, to flourish, in this world—to balance and complement.

If we're stuck in a state of too much doing, we forget how to simply *be*, which is unhealthy and leads to unhappiness. We lack a sense of meaning. Conversely, if we're consistently in a state of "being," we may be living a life that almost entirely resides in our head and may not be manifesting real change in our world.

Our society often portrays us as one-dimensional, and that dimension tends to be only physical, masculine. That needs to change. Both aspects need to be valued. Both are important for overall balance.

Feminine power first begins with an increased sense of presence. It requires you to be able, at any given moment, to know who you are and how you're feeling. What can you bring to the table at this moment? What can you *reasonably* offer? Are you feeling afraid? Confused? Or are you in a state of love? Courage? Light and compassion?

Once you recognize your genuine state of being, it begins to impact everything around you. Essentially, you're checking in with yourself and then making a move (doing) from that place. You're not forcing yourself to act from a place of guilt or obligation. You're not disconnected from your real feelings or trying too hard to please others. You recognize your true essence first. Then you can act in the world from a more authentic framework.

What Makes a Woman Powerful

(Hint: It's not the red dress.)

The word "feminine" often elicits a picture of a perfect-looking woman in high heels, lipstick and a flowery dress. That is *not* what I'm talking about.

Femininity is a state of being. You could wear plain old jeans and a t-shirt and be incredibly feminine. On the flip side, you could rock a figure-hugging red dress and stiletto heels and not be in alignment with your feminine side. It depends on the energy you're bringing, not the clothes you're wearing.

This idea clicked for me at an event several years ago hosted by well-known motivational guru Tony Robbins.

Tony asked all the ladies who wanted to dance on the stage to come on down. The ballroom was packed with over 3,000 people. Half of us were women. We obviously were not all going to fit on the stage, so only the bravest and most assertive would make it. (At least that's what I told myself.)

I was sitting fairly far away from the stage in an assigned seat, so if I wanted to be one of the dancers, I was going to have to hurry up and run as fast as I could. As much as I wanted to go, however, my feet would not move. Though I'd always had a love affair with dancing, I was petrified.

Sounds paradoxical, huh? Here's the truth: although I loved dancing and it was the one thing that made me feel alive, I was also very self-conscious about my physical attributes (like being overweight) and quite often would let my feelings of inadequacy stop me from pursuing what was most important to me—like dancing.

What if I make a fool out of myself? What if people start laughing at me?

Apparently the critic in my head was still ruling my life. More debilitating thoughts emerged: *Besides, I'm too fat. Better leave the stage for the pretty girls. No one would understand my dancing anyway.*

My passion for dancing started when I was a little girl. I have always taken dance classes. But dance classes, much like dance clubs, weren't enough for me. For me, dancing is a deep spiritual experience. One with the potential to connect me directly with my soul.

I wanted to take this dancing experience further and share it with the world, but I consistently got in my own way. That little, nagging voice always showed up at the most inconvenient times. Now once again, just at the time I was seeking transformation, it had the power to keep me still. I passed on the opportunity, once again, to share of myself. The stage was full and I wasn't on it.

Part of me was actually relieved, especially when I heard Tony say that there was going to be a contest: after the ladies danced on stage, all the gentlemen would vote for who was the sexiest. *What?!? Boy, am I glad I didn't go up there. I'm not sexy. I'm thirty pounds overweight!*

Tony signaled for the music, and the contest began. There must have been thirty or forty women on stage, but there was only room for around six in the front row. Competition was fierce. *These ladies are not playing around!* They were willing to do anything to take the spotlight, including pushing each other around or "dirty dancing." I felt myself getting more and more annoyed. *This is b.s.! I didn't come here for this! I thought this was going to be a transformational event! Besides, it's obvious that the pretty blonde girl in the short red dress is going to win.*

Then Tony stopped the music. He noticed a chubby young woman being pushed toward the back of the stage. I wasn't sure why he was so interested in her. She looked simple, plain. He brought her to the front of the stage and let the music continue.

As I had expected, after a couple of minutes, the ruthless ladies had once again pushed the chubby young woman to the back. To be honest, I didn't notice her very much. She wasn't ugly. Actually, after looking at her more closely, I realized she was quite pretty, although she didn't seem to give her appearance much thought. In fact, it was hard to notice her with her bare skin, old jeans, and plain t-shirt.

Tony stopped the music again. He cracked a joke about how aggressive the ladies in the front were and how they were pushing everyone out of their way. Again, he brought the plain young woman back out to the front and began the voting process. He asked the men to clap for the woman they thought was the sexiest. (He asked the ladies in the audience to simply watch and not participate. He claimed to already know what our opinion would be. *Of course,* I thought, *it's the little blonde with the tiny red dress.*)

He proceeded to place his hand on top of each woman's head and asked the men to vote. First up was the most aggressive one, who had pushed everyone to the back in order to make room for her gymnastic moves. The response was small; very little clapping came from the men. Even though she was quite pretty, I wasn't too surprised.

The next two women got a similar response. He then went up to the beautiful blonde girl. I felt a rush of jealousy come over me, followed by a wave of shame for being jealous. *What am I doing? I should know better than that!* He placed his hand over her head ... and there were hardly any claps! *Huh??? WTF?* I was stunned!

The blonde girl looked as stunned as I was. She had clearly invested hours of time in her appearance. Everything was exactly as she thought it should be: perfectly combed long blonde hair, check; red manicured nails, check; flawless makeup, check; tight, sexy red dress, check; red stiletto shoes, check. So what was missing? It couldn't have been her dancing; she'd been showing off her sexy curves and dancing as erotically as her four-inch heels had allowed.

Then Tony placed his hand above the head of the plain young woman. *The room went wild.* All the men in the room were clapping and whistling for this shy girl in jeans and a t-shirt. I was so confused. *Was this a conspiracy? Did all the men get together and decide to play a trick on us? Did she have some special moves that I didn't notice?*

She did seem sweet, someone I could even hang out with and call my friend. She actually even reminded me of ... *me!* Humble, modest, shy, not very sure of herself, the complete opposite of vain ... but *sexy???* The unassuming woman also seemed to be confused by the applause and burst into tears. Tony turned to us and began to explain what had just happened. What followed was the greatest lesson I'd ever heard on being a woman:

No matter how much we have evolved as human beings, there are still things that are natural to women and other things that are natural to men.

Feminine energy is moved mostly by emotions; it's about opening to love and giving love. Masculine energy is primarily driven by directions in life and by a life mission. Feminine essence feels a need to fill itself up with love, energy and attention; it wants to feel understood. Masculine essence, on the other hand, responds to challenges, loves competition, and thrives on solving problems; it wants to feel appreciated. Repressing your own nature will only lead to frustration and lack of fulfillment.

Sometimes women dress provocatively because we feel a need to call attention to ourselves; we want validation and approval. It comes from a place of neediness, and it ends up being, to some extent, manipulative. It is also a masculine trait. So on some level, you're being masculine while wearing a woman's outfit...like that woman in the red dress.

Tools for Connecting to Your Feminine Power

A short while after that event, I really started on my journey of self-discovery. I began to ask myself, "Okay, what do I need to go further? I don't want complicated, fancy formulas to process and remember. I can't deal with that. What are simple points I can return to easily?"

And that's how *The Five Feminine Power Virtues* was born. It offers five accessible states of being that naturally bolster our feminine side and allow us to reconnect with our essence.

- Presence
- Authenticity
- Sensuality
- Spirituality
- Gratitude

Presence. We often get stuck in the trap of multitasking. It's still a challenge for me every day. And that's all right… it happens in today's fast-paced world. But it's necessary to recommit yourself to total presence and focus on one thing at a time. When you're aware of the present moment, you are living more consciously and fully. You're raising your consciousness and becoming more aware of why you're doing the things you're doing. Without this awareness, we can often find ourselves on "automatic" and feel disconnected.

Meditation and prayer are both excellent methods of becoming more present. But ultimately, we want our *entire existence* to be rooted in a state of presence, not just fifteen minutes of pillow-sitting. We want to go through life open-eyed, aware. It's the only way to fully thrive spiritually.

Authenticity. It sounds like a weighty word but the concept is essentially basic. In it's simplest terms, it means being who you are.

Are you in alignment with your values and desires?

Are you being true to yourself?

Are you allowing yourself to fully "be" in this world without apology or shame?

Authenticity can be tricky for women because we're bombarded with so many different messages from the media. We're not quite sure what defines our own particular brand of authenticity. And sorting out what you were *taught* to believe from what you *really* believe can be a long process.

So finding your truth takes some soul-searching. What's important to remember is this: there is no *one* truth. There is only *your* truth. It's your responsibility to discover your authenticity. (No one else can do it!)

Sensuality. No, we're not talking about bedroom-variety sexuality here. Sensuality consists of what pleasurably relates to your senses, with or without another person. Sensuality reflects your level of joy and pleasure in the world (again, not just in bed).

When we're consistently deprived of sensual pleasure and locked in "doing" mode, sooner or later we experience burnout. So sensuality is *critical* for women.

Sensuality can be boosted by anything from listening to music and moving your hips (a powerful area on a woman's body) to a hot bath to a soothing cup of tea to a warm embrace with a lover. You simply need to seek out sensual experiences in your everyday life. (They're all around you and don't require a visit to the spa!)

What is giving you sensual comfort right now?

What makes you feel tingling and alive?

What senses are your strongest?

What would your ultimate sensual experience be like?

How about your environment? Does it speak to your sensual side? This could mean anything from bright colors on your walls to a soft, comforting blanket to a rocking chair that fits your body just right.

Remember this: your sensuality shouldn't be reliant on another person. You can enhance this state of being whenever you'd like, since so many sensual opportunities surround you. But you *do* need to consistently make it happen. *Sensual maintenance is required!*

Spirituality. This simply means a *connection* with a higher being and a deep knowing that you're not alone. We're *naturally* spiritual beings and require that "big connection" in order to thrive, just like we need to eat food and drink water.

And we're not talking religion. Religion and spirituality can be two *radically* different experiences! Religion is a human-made social structure, whereas spirituality is an intimate feeling that there's something greater than us. (I often joke that spirituality is the direct hook-up and religion is more of a middleman.)

But we all must connect with our higher being on our *own* terms. Spirituality is as personal as our thumbprint. Our "gods" can vary drastically...and that's okay. It's more than okay—our different takes on spirituality need to be *celebrated*.

Gratitude. This virtue is the glue that ties all of the other virtues together. At this point, most of us have heard (perhaps too much) about gratitude. Yet we often continue to be "thankful" from a "should" place; we feel *obligated* to be grateful for the gifts in our lives.

But gratitude is so much more. When you are in a state of gratitude, you're living in a higher vibration. And that impacts everything and everyone around us. It's a powerful force, not just an obligatory list you jot down at bedtime.

And yes, we *all* struggle with gratitude when things are not going our way. Unfortunately or not, these are the moments it's the *most* important to be grateful. Even during hard times, we can dig deep and be thankful for the meaning to be found in those challenges. We can be grateful for the blessings that abound, even during our darkest nights.

Not easy, I know. But that's the spiritual challenge we're here to face. Because when we live in a state of gratitude, our whole life opens up.

Dropping the Role of Superwoman & Putting Ourselves First

Another way women disconnect from their natural feminine essence is by overdoing. Somehow, we equate busyness with womanhood. But constantly doing for others is a sure way to deplete your energy and have nothing left for yourself. We all know the signs. We feel exhausted, drained, overwhelmed…very disconnected.

I often joke with my friends when I'm stuck in the act of overdoing. I say, "Oh I forgot…I'm not superwoman" because I, like many others, struggle with this tendency. But now when I see those telltale signs—exhaustion, confusion, a sense of being overwhelmed—I stop and regroup. Taking care of myself *has* to be my first priority. We need to drop the role of superwomen and remember to sometimes put ourselves first.

I find that when women overdo, they do so from a place of inferiority—as if everyone else matters first. If there's a hierarchy, they are at the bottom desperately trying to work their way up. Everyone above them holds more importance.

But when we put people above us, we have trouble accepting character flaws or imperfections in them. Often, we then end up throwing the baby out with the bathwater and getting rid of these people completely when we are finally confronted with these flaws. Or we secretly feel anger that they aren't who we thought they'd be. *The sad part?* We miss out on the *beauty* of imperfection. We miss out on the offerings people have to give us, even though they're humanly imperfect.

The takeaway lesson—and one of the keys to the return of your feminine truth—is that the more you accept your own imperfections, the more you give others a break. The more you're able to take care of yourself, the more you're ultimately able to give others—not just directly, but through your influence and leadership.

Our New Role as Women

Women are tremendous influencers and leaders. The unfortunate part is that we often downplay these traits or fail to recognize their importance. And it's a shame because we utilize these traits every day, whether we are soccer moms or high-powered businesswomen.

On a daily basis, we serve as sources of inspiration, as influencers, as leaders, and as healers. Women are the lightworkers of the world and we have the capacity to *share* that light. Together, we can eradicate the darkness around us … and in *ourselves*.

We're at a stage at which it's *very* important to create a balance in our shared consciousness. Feminism is tremendously important in its own right. But we had to fight its way into existence. And any time a revolution of that magnitude takes place, the pendulum can swing too far in one direction. We needed those masculine traits in order to make change, but we *still* need a balance to thrive in the future.

Dalai Lama once said, "The world will be saved by the Western woman." And that has always resonated with me. The world *will* be saved by women...Western and otherwise. We will be saved *collectively* by reconnecting with our feminine truths—both men and women need to undergo this transformation for a global change to occur.

I talk at length about this in my book, *The Five Feminine Power Virtues*. Women need to gather forces, forge a community, and leverage the power of that group. It's time stop the backbiting and gossiping and bickering.

As females, we are natural connectors and we need to return to that state. A community is critical to our growth. But that masculine mentality based on competition and "winning" steers us away from our natural, community-based place of strength.

Now let me clarify: there's nothing inherently wrong with competition. Most of us understand that there are healthy forms of competition that help us achieve our goals. But we're often *consumed* by it instead of working with it in doses. We feel our very identity is based on a million different ways in which we "win" or "lose."

So search out and join communities that inspire you. Practice opening your heart to other women, even when old insecurities rise up. Share your heart in face of your fears—that's real courage. That's *feminine* courage. Because when you do open up in this way, you open your heart to yourself as well. You're ultimately reconnecting with yourself by reaching out and being present for others.

The Final Challenge, the Big Picture

The final (perhaps biggest) challenge we face is simply recognizing the power we *already* possess. We're so preoccupied caring for others or trying to win approval or competing that we don't know how to tap into that quiet, feminine side, full of strength and beauty. *And she's been there the whole time.*

It's also key to remember that the woman you are, right now, *is* enough. *More* than enough. It's that elegantly simple.

Reconnecting with my feminine side has drastically changed my life. I feel more relaxed, in tune and in charge. It's a whole new and magical state of being, almost hard to explain in words.

When I started this process, I was like many other women, endlessly juggling, spiritually and sensually depleted, chasing after goals that weren't truly mine, and looking for answers everywhere else but inside of me. Trust me, I've been through it! And breaking free from the roles we've been auto-playing is no easy process. (The world doesn't always support your journey, unfortunately!)

Though it's been a long and winding road, I wouldn't have had it any other way. I discovered there's another way to exist in this world as a woman—a more authentic and powerful state of being that feels in complete alignment with who I truly am.

> *"The woman's mission is not to enhance the masculine spirit, but to express the feminine; hers is not to preserve a man-made world, but to create a human world by the infusion of the feminine element into all of its activities."*
> – MARGARET THATCHER

CHAPTER 2

Gina Cloud

Gina Cloud is a passionate W.O.M.A.N., deeply devoted teacher, author, creator of GinaCology, speaker, life coach, women's health expert, dancer, and single mother of a daughter. She has spent the last 25 years developing her body of work based on the powerful biological cycles of women's lives, through her own personal journey into self-mastery and the idea that women can and do heal themselves. Gina teaches women the powerful and unique language of their bodies as a path for transformation, and the outcome is deep and beautiful in the areas of self-love, self-respect, self-esteem, and self-confidence, all through the powerful medium of the Feminine. She believes that if you can't love your body - as a power source-then you can't love your life.

Gina has been a guest on many radio programs, and is the former host of her own radio show, GinaCology, which can be found on iTunes. Gina published her first book: W.O.M.A.N., A New Definition in 2009. She has been a guest expert on The Ricki Lake Show on the topic of body image and self-esteem and has appeared on various news and TV programs related to women's issues Learn more at http://www.ginacloud.com.

My Story and My Journey to Power

I am a mother, author, speaker, teacher, mentor, coach, dancer, W.O.M.A.N., rebel, and change-maker. When people ask what got me to this present moment in my life, I tell them I've been driven by questions and my body has been my tour guide. Many people's stories reveal a hardship or a tragedy that took them down the road of healing, leading them to their life's work, but that is not my tale. My story is one of rebellion and having the courage necessary to trust the voice within myself. It's about my refusal to allow external influences to dictate my own truths and instead choosing to listen to my own intuition. It's about a young girl who couldn't ask "Why?" enough times and found that if the answer didn't ring true within herself, she could not accept it.

Everything of value I have ever learned, I learned from my body. My body has been my compass, my wise mentor, my healer, and my initiating force. My inner voice has always been louder than the ones I've heard around me, including those of my parents, teachers, "authorities" of all kinds, and most generally accepted rules and beliefs. This doesn't mean that I was reckless and never listened; it just seemed that my intuition was so aligned with my one and only indubitable truth that its bullshit meter was flawless. I believe that there's THE truth—my truth and your truth. We all know THE truth when we hear it. It hits you in the heart.

I grew up with very old-school definitions of gender roles. My father was sexist and didn't believe in women being equal to men, and because I spoke out against his perspective, the subject was a hotbed of debate between us. My mother was basically voiceless, submissive not by choice but from lack of connection to her own power, so I had no real model for how to be a woman. Though this was a source of angst for me in my young adult years, I ultimately recognized it to be a gift, as I was able to decide how I wanted to define *myself* as a woman.

I found myself guided by my own questions: *What does it mean to be a woman? What does it mean to be in my power? Where does my power come from? How do I use my power? How is my power different from men's? What other messages am I getting about being a woman in the world?* As I looked around for answers to these questions, I observed so much conformity around gender and power. Everything I saw reinforced suffocating definitions on both men and women and promoted the idea that somehow women were weak or less than men—an idea that was completely unacceptable to me. I *knew* this idea was wrong and I refused to accept it. I knew these biological, sociological, and personal perceptions were NOT the truth, but rather myths we had all bought into collectively. As these questions began to drive my life, I learned that the questions we ask are more important than the answers we ultimately find, as the questions lead you on the journey. The journey is how we grow, evolve, and expand.

When I was fourteen, I began to truly connect with my feminine power. Getting my first period opened a door for me to what would become a lifelong fascination, education, and passion. It was a turning point. The biological differences that had always fascinated me about men and women took on a different meaning as I began to understand the power inherent in a woman's body. Though I'd grown up hearing nothing but negativity about the menstrual cycle from my mother and every other woman who had anything to say about it, I will never forget the magic and power I felt when I got mine. I felt *superhuman*—like I could see through walls and had the power to *sense* and *know* everything.

That feeling has remained with me throughout my entire life. And so my driving question became: *How could I be the only woman in the world who felt this way?*

The answer to that question seemed, to me, obvious: *I am not the only one.*

I have always understood that this knowledge has been gifted to me. I am, in essence, a channel. Wisdom comes *through* me as I listen beyond my own mind and allow my body to guide the ride, and I am just here to help other women remember their power through their bodies.

And so my journey into the mysteries of the female body began. Though I initially focused on the menstrual cycle, my journey later grew to encompass ALL of the rites of passage that are unique to women: menstruation, pregnancy/birth, and menopause. As I immersed myself in the experience of being in a woman's body, I began to understand the nature and power of being a woman. Unfortunately, we exist in a world where women are constantly attacked, shamed, maligned, and dishonored through our bodies. We devalue the most important teacher we will ever have, disconnecting from the wisdom contained within it. Women are not taught to *know* that our bodies are in many ways the SOURCE of our power. The more we listen to and believe the noise about what—according to the media, medicine, and society at large—is "wrong" with us, the less we learn about this powerful truth and our ability to put it to use in our lives.

How I Define Power

For me, power is not the male model of dominion, or power *over*, but rather power *from within*. It is the power to emanate, to radiate, to be magnetic, and to generate. It is also the ability to surrender, which is anchored in the heart. For me, this power comes from being centered in my heart and being aligned with my body. When I am in those two places together, the wisdom that comes through *is* the power. I believe that the greatest journey we ever take in life is the one that leads from the head to the heart. In the head, what we know is knowledge, but when it arrives at our hearts, it is wisdom. When I live my life from such a model, the wisdom that pours in from that connection really is powerful. It's in my presence, in what I emanate, in my conviction, and in my voice, my truth, and my integrity. It's in how I care for other people and in how I love, value, and honor myself. *That's* power and that, specifically, is what makes a woman powerful. That feminine energy is the energy and essence of creation. It is an emanation from within—subtle, yet more powerful than any external force.

I believe that if men walked through life with a sense of power from within rather than embracing the notion of power over, it would be a very different world and humanity would in many ways be more united than divided. I have learned in my journey that the alignment of those polarities, of masculine and feminine within each of us, is our key to harmony as individuals, and in the world by extension. Men often fear their inner feminine energy, as they, too, believe the precepts they have been taught— that all things female are weak and inferior. As they resist their own wise inner feminine voice, choosing rather to suppress and vilify it within themselves, this suppression and vilification also becomes projected outward onto women in the world. I believe one of the major causes of violence towards women is men's lack of alignment with and refusal to embrace their inner feminine energy. If men could honor and support their inner feminine in allegiance with their outer masculine, they would revere and support actual women and the feminine principle on earth.

What Makes a Woman Powerful

It seems to me that many women move about the world emulating the maddening corporate-type male models of power. We are trying to *become* powerful, rather than *being in* our power. Chasing power will not bring it to you. Generally, and collectively, we believe that being female is less than being male, so we strive to become more male. *What would happen if women could embrace these softer places that really embody strength and power in the most fundamental ways? What if we stopped allowing the exploitation and denigration of women's bodies? What if we shed our beliefs around all things female being weak? What if we stopped trying to follow these current models and allowed our own authentic ones to evolve?* A powerful woman embraces her biology and her psychology as strength rather than weakness, and does not feel inferior for having periods, becoming pregnant, or going through menopause. This triad of uniquely female experiences is a large part of *why* we are powerful as women. When we negate these experiences or try to suppress them, we are embracing the concept that we are flawed *because* we are women. Our biology defines so much of our lives for the entirety of our lives, so how could it not be an inherent aspect of female power? If you are having an *aha* moment or formulating a thought-provoking question as you read these words, that is YOUR inner wisdom reaching out to you.

Feminism is not where we are now. I believe we are now in a place of reclaiming an important element that feminism removed from our lives. While it strives to give us equality in the economic world, it has also created an ideology around suppressing what defines us as females in the world, teaching us to become as much like men as possible in order to be treated fairly, equally, and with respect. Ironically, feminism, despite its many gifts, also inadvertently created the masculinization of many women by embracing society's underlying belief that our biology was our downfall. I do believe feminism serves an important purpose, and I consider myself a feminist, but I also recognize that it has created sameness rather than equality. Many women have learned to suppress what is feminine within them because the world has become an unsafe environment for its expression, given our current climate of violence against women. But we must find the courage to bring it forth and use it to heal ourselves individually and collectively and to restore the balance of masculine and feminine here on planet Earth.

I mentioned surrender and vulnerability as an aspect of feminine power, but I speak of it as an individual choice, not as something that is forced upon you. When we choose to surrender, we open our hearts and minds to receive the wisdom of our intuitive inner voices. That voice is one I have always listened to and always will (no matter how crazy She may sound at times). I have found that when we are not aligned with our biology, we close much of our access to this voice, as it penetrates us most powerfully when we are attuned to our biological rhythms. If men are not aligned with their inner feminine and women are out of alignment with their inner and outer feminine, where is the feminine power to be found? It is up to us to restore the collective balance by first restoring it within ourselves. I am here to remind you that having a woman's body is an extraordinary gift and an immense blessing. It's time for us to reclaim this gift and blessing.

Tools for Connecting to Your Feminine Power

I teach women the powerful and unique language of their bodies as a path for transformation and use many tools to help them achieve this reconnection. Here, I will share just a few of the ones I find most powerful. Most importantly, I have ten *GinaCology* Principles that will lead you to balance in all areas of your life as a woman. You can find them all on my website at *www.ginacloud.com*.

First and foremost: *be in your body*. Do things that will connect you with it. Your body and your emotions are inextricably intertwined, and no one will ever be able to convince me that our cycles and our psyches are not in perfect partnership. For women still menstruating, get to know your cycle. I teach an entire series on this topic alone. It is so rich, deep, beautiful, and life affirming. It is the wisdom and the reminder that we are aligned with nature and that our bodies are microcosms of the macrocosms of the earth. What a woman's body goes through in terms of her cycle is very much an equivalent of what the earth goes through. I have renamed our menstrual cycle *The Sacred Cycle* because it is one of the greatest teachers and healers that we possess and one that allows you to be in constant integrity with yourself. Rather than using the negatively branded term "PMS," I choose to call it **P**owerful **M**onthly **S**ight. Pay attention to what surfaces right *before* your bleeding starts. That week before is your truth.

During this time, you can't b.s. yourself regarding what you "make nice" about the rest of the month. If you can make time for even a day of what I call *seclusion ritual*, you will find the truth, *your* truth, more than during any other time of the month. It is in that stillness and surrender that you can truly feel what is not working for you and where you're lying to yourself and hiding from any number of issues in your life, from your relationships to your job to your life course. Your cycle is your best friend, bar none. If, on the other hand, you leave these issues unattended to, ignored, or suppressed, you will have terrible PMS of the raging, traditionally mainstream kind.

Align yourself with your own personal rhythm, and your life will change RADICALLY. I can guarantee it. I've worked with many, many women whose lives have been changed forever by observing this simple practice.

I also teach women to become "self-centered." Yes, that's right, centered in yourself. Not to be *selfish*, as that word is commonly used, but rather to put yourself first on your to-do list. I've been a single mother since my daughter was five, and she's twenty years old now. I have had to work full time at another job to pay the bills while juggling my passion, and it has been challenging. Through these experiences, I have learned this tenet. In doing my dharma, I teach what I'm living and I share what I'm going through. Being CENTERED IN YOURSELF bestows power. There is no way that we can joyfully do all that we must if we don't choose to nurture ourselves first. You're going to be stressed, frustrated, depressed, angry and empty. I have learned to tell my daughter, "If I'm ever yelling at you or giving you a hard time, I want you to do me a favor: Look at me, stop me, and ask me, *'Mom, when was the last time you did something for yourself?'"* If you have children, teach them to ask you this. When you hear those words, something incredible happens—the question will bring you home to an honest realization. And if you don't have kids, teach your significant other to ask it.

I have learned that when I have neglected my need for whatever makes me feel full and content, it's impossible to really *give* in all the ways that I desire. We are all the same in this. It's very much like the instructions we receive on an airplane before takeoff about the oxygen masks and remembering to put on your own before helping others. Being self-centered allows you to live and give much more than you can imagine, and to do it all with a heart full of love.

Another vital tool is for women to honor their sexuality and allow it to be expressed AUTHENTICALLY. Women's sexuality is not the same as men's, yet again we are constantly attempting to keep up with how men "do sex." There is a huge level of dissatisfaction among women regarding their sex lives, and I believe this to be an important awakening. It's the collective unconsciousness of women saying a loud "no" to the violent sexual climate we live in. We must step in and create a necessary change.

Our sexuality as women is a potent and vital force in our lives. Many women have given up on trying to have what they want sexually. Many women can't even discuss the topic and feel there is something wrong WITH THEM, rather than trusting that what their body wisdom is saying to them about sex is THE truth. Many women don't have a relationship with their sexuality, due in large or small part to a disconnection from their bodies. Regardless of the "why," our sexuality is a vital and juicy (pun intended) aspect of our power as women, and it's time we reclaim it. We must have integrity around our sexuality and what that means, as well as our ability to be able to express and own it, FULLY AND FREELY. We must reclaim OUR sexuality as distinct, potent, and separate from men's expectations of us. And we must disassociate from the notion that if we don't "do sex" for men the way they want it, we won't be desired or loved.

There is a huge difference between sexy and sensual. Sexy is a doing thing, while sensual is a *being* thing. Reclaim your sensuality by learning to love your body. Give yourself permission to say "yes" to what you want and "no" to what genuinely doesn't feel right to you, without self-judgment and without giving a damn about how you may be perceived. Be present in your body and learn how to tap into the wisdom and teachings that are there every single day for you. If you give yourself the time, faith, and openness to surrender to your authentic truth, you'll find it there. And remember, if you can't love your body—not in its appearance, but as a power source—you can't love your life. One of my favorite quotes that speaks to this is by Simone de Beauvoir: "To lose confidence in one's body is to lose confidence in one's self."

One of my most favorite tools is dance. As you read this, if you're a woman who loves dance and does it often, you know *exactly* what I mean. If you love dance but don't do it anymore, you also know what I mean because you will remember how it aligned you with your own energy centers, the flow of the feminine, the softness and playfulness of woman, and the sensuality that is vital to our essence. If you've never danced, or are afraid to because you think you can't, don't know how, or have some judgment about your "abilities," then you, most of all, need to give yourself this gift. When I say dance is vital, I am not exaggerating. All women can dance. It's a matter of surrendering to the rhythm you are listening to, whether it's actual music, your inner sense of "music," or that of nature. It's not about technique. I encourage all women to dance at least a couple times a week— you can even do it in your own home if you can't get out. Light a candle, take off your clothes, and move! Move your emotions through your body. Move your joy, your sexuality, your anger, frustration, or sadness...whatever you are holding onto. Choose music that suits your most blocked feeling. For instance, I have pieces of music that *always* make me cry, so when I feel stuck emotionally and know I need to cry but can't, I will use those pieces of music to get myself going and unstop the dam. There's never a time that this tool doesn't work. When you move your body, your life moves with you. Whatever is happening within you will also be manifested in your external life. So if you used to dance and don't anymore, or never have, add it to that to-do list I mentioned earlier and prioritize it for yourself, whether you go to a class, do it at home, or go out. And dance naked periodically. It's a beautiful kind of liberation for any woman's soul.

Another all-encompassing tool for women is to live life as a W.O.M.A.N. This is an acronym, the title of my book, and one of my *GinaCology* Principles. The letters stand for W.ild, O.pen, M.agical, A.uthentically-Empowered, N.ectar. This redefinition is the heart and soul of much of my work and has become my manifesto.

W.ild is the instinctual, primal connection to ourselves that we have all but lost today, and inherent in it is our connection to our authentic sexuality without apology, as I mentioned earlier.

Our Wildness is a vital aspect that's been suppressed for millennia in women. We've been shamed, demonized, and burned at the stake for this aspect of who we are. And so we have repressed Her. She is also the bold, brazen, fearless aspect of every woman. Letting "HER" out of the box will save your soul and reinvigorate your life.

O.pen is about living through our hearts with vulnerability, embracing compassion for oneself and others, and surrendering to our inner voice and its infallible GPS (Goddess Power Source). Without this piece, we stay fully immersed in the masculine paradigm, which is heart-protective. Our openness as women is one of our gifts, as the heart and the womb are interconnected. I refer to our uterus as the "lower heart." When our upper and lower hearts are connected and communicating, we as women are THE POWER of life, as creation (womb) and love (heart) aligned. I have learned in my own life that this sacred alignment of heart and womb is the most vital of connections we have access to, and it belongs only to woman.

M.agical refers to our biological processes and the wisdom we learn through our bodies. I spoke earlier about the menstrual cycle, which is not only a *huge* piece of our guidance system, but also an extraordinary rite of passage. We are also blessed with many teachings and gifts through pregnancy and birth. Yet so many women are being robbed of these experiences in a culture micromanaged by the western medical paradigm, one that reinforces the myth that women should not trust their bodies. This same paradigm has influenced many women to believe that menopause is the end of your life, vitality and beauty. In truth, menopause is actually the beginning of coming into your FULL power as a woman. It is a time when the portals for access to power, deeper wisdom, freedom, and self-love are wide open. If we were to view this rite of passage for what it truly is, women's lives would change forever. When we change our perceptions, we change our reality.

A.uthentically-Empowered is the taking of your own unique gifts, fully turned on, and giving them to the world, expressed through your work. It is finding a way to live it out loud and proud while gifting it to as many people as you can. And yes, getting paid for doing what you love. If you're in a job that isn't honoring you, begin to examine how you can change this to be aligned with who you know you really are.

Nectar is the beautiful, soft, still, playful, dancing, sensual, lighthearted, colorful, laughing aspect of W.O.M.A.N. It's a side of us we rarely experience because it requires us to *be* and to stop all the doing. It requires us to surrender and listen to our inner desires and what makes us feel joyful. Finding activities that activate these qualities for you will greatly enhance your life and your sense of both inner and outer power in your life.

Our New Role as Women and Our Challenges

Being a woman today requires blending past roles with new ones we are co-creating. I believe that women can and will heal the planet at this point in our evolution as a species. Until we can respect ourselves and step firmly into all aspects of ourselves as women—embracing both inner and outer power—nothing will change. There's so much chaos on the planet everywhere, and violence seems to be permeating everything. The earth is being raped constantly and more violently than ever, and so are women.

Despite and because of this, we have to be willing to trust the softer heart aspect of who we are and step into that vulnerability, listening and leading as a force. I believe our biggest challenge is our own fear of the feminine energy that we each carry. It's institutionalized and woven into every fiber of society and fully anchored into our beliefs about ourselves. We've undergone an epic brainwashing, and I see our reclaiming our bodies as the key to unlocking the prison door. I believe this to be one of those truths that belong to us all. I have experienced it in my own life and feel it is my destiny to help other women awaken to this knowledge.

From girlhood, consciously and unconsciously, females are taught by society to be focused *against* alignment in our bodies, so that women and girls spend an inordinate amount of their lives obsessing about body weight and physical appearance. I see this as a distraction from our true power and gifts. And we have bought into it so fully, particularly in terms of our values around reproductive health, the fashion and beauty industry, and the anti-aging market. When we believe our value and worth is only on the outside, we cannot awaken to know that what we house within us is far more valuable, potent, and needed—by ourselves individually and by the world. In addition, our sexuality has been used to hold us hostage, and the masculine's pursuit of owning our bodies belies a truth we are unwilling to see: that what we posses is *valuable* and goes far beyond what is between our legs. It's time we open our eyes and tune into who we really are and the power that we possess in and through these bodies that are capable of magical feats.

I also believe strongly that we *need* a community of women who are like-minded and who are able to support each other.

We love to collaborate, to do things together, and to support one another. We try to do too much alone and burn out, but when two or more women come together for a cause, watch out! We are an unstoppable force, especially when driven by our hearts. Overcoming this challenge will require conscious effort to find those other like-minded women, but more than ever, we are looking for and finding each other. I think we are often more willing to commit to a cause much larger than ourselves than to a small one in the realm of our personal lives. We need to be able to surrender to needing and ASKING for help. We need to be able to say, *"You know what, I need some help. Can you support me?"*

For many women, one of the biggest challenges will be using their voices, speaking up, speaking out, taking a stand, and saying what's so, rather than what someone else wants to hear (also known as being "nice"). I also see as an important challenge the need to bring men into this new paradigm without alienating them. Their model for power is exclusive and competitive. Ours is inclusive and communal. Throughout history, men have feared female power, which has led to our being repressed and suppressed in many ways. One of the most important tasks we currently have before us is to lead in a way that empowers us all. For this, we will need our strong, clear, bold voices, our open hearts, and each other's support. We need to enlist men in this cause because without their support, this is an uphill battle.

There are many, many conscious men aligned with this cause and we need them. The goal is not to shift the balance of power over to the feminine in suppression of the masculine. We know all too well that repression is not the answer. We must teach by example with wisdom and grace. It is our time to become power-filled agents of change in whatever areas of life we are called to.

And most of all, on a daily basis, we need to honor and value what we see when we look in the mirror and celebrate *all* that we are, body, mind, heart and soul. We are truly exquisite.

CHAPTER 3

Katie Day

 *Since 1989 Katie has followed her passion of working with women. She works with organizations, influencing change, and externally via her training programs. Katie has witnessed thousands of women evolve to become the women they were born to be. Her signature training program is The High-heeled Leader, Step into your Spotlight and Shine, supported by her book, The High-heeled Leader.*

Katie has run her signature session, The Top Ten Skills for Women in Business, across the world including India, Dubai and Kenya.

Katie has appeared on Radio in the UK, US and Australia, and on TV in Canada and Dubai speaking on women in business. Her articles have featured in many global business publications. Katie is a regular journalist for The Huffington Post, Women Unlimited, Prowess and Project Eve.

Katie's message is: 'Franks Fools Crows, Lakota Sioux Chief, said "The 21st Century will see an era of peace and prosperity, and it will be brought in my women." Very sensible man was Frank – let's prove him right!' Find out about Katie's programs at www.thehighheeledleader.com.

My Story and My Journey to Power

I don't know who said, "If you want to make God laugh, make a plan," but it's so true. I have learnt the most important life lessons from unpredictable experiences and circumstances. In fact, my life has tended to work better when I haven't tried to control it. Whether these experiences are positive or negative, it is our reactions to them that determine who we will become in the future.

Embracing my inner power of being a woman in the world came about as a direct result of my experiencing bad relationships. Once I recognized that I had attracted these relationships into my life because of how I then viewed myself, I finally began to make internal changes. Acknowledging that I had not taken true ownership of my feminine power allowed me to see that these relationships had been a necessary part of my journey and self-actualization. Though these experiences were challenging and personally traumatic, without them I may never have fully stepped into my feminine power. I might have coasted through life, continuing to attract the wrong energy—and therefore the wrong man—into my life, which inevitably would have chipped away at, and finally destroyed, my feminine power.

My personal breakdown began when I was in my early thirties. By this time I had been married and divorced twice. I was thirty-one and just coming out of divorce number two. There was a moment when I was sitting in my home feeling very sorry for myself and thinking, "Why do I keep attracting the wrong man? What have they all got in common?" Then it dawned on me, the common denominator was...me!

Whilst it was hard to admit that I was partially at fault—that the blame didn't all fall on these men—doing so was also liberating. As a result of this self-honesty, I felt myself move from "victim" state to "powerful feminine" state. I needed to take full ownership of who I was as a woman in the world—to take ownership of my journey and tackle the limiting self-beliefs I was currently holding on to. I saw with startling clarity that these past relationships had simply been a reflection of how I'd viewed myself at that time. I had been inviting back into my aura the energy I was radiating out into the world about my personal view of "me." These men had been simply reflecting my beliefs about myself and confirming my view of how I felt as a woman in the world at that time. If I wanted different relationships, the first relationship I needed to change was the one I had with myself. *I had to love, honor and respect me before I could expect anyone else to love, honor, and respect me.*

One of my favorite quotes is from Eleanor Roosevelt: "No one can make you feel inferior without your consent." I use this quote when I am training and working with women as a reminder that we have the power to create our realities and our lives. The key that unlocked the door for me to step into my magnificence as a woman was the acknowledgement of my role in my past experiences; once I had acknowledged and accepted my role, I was able to make the necessary changes. We can't change what we're not aware of! Acceptance and honesty are crucial to the success of the manifestation of feminine power.

I grew up with low self-esteem. I was an overweight child and teenager, which resulted in my having an eating disorder at the age of seventeen. My parents split up when I was nine years old, after which I didn't see my father for two years. Mum and I had some exceptionally challenging times when we were on our own, including being homeless. I was bullied at school and, when I did finally start seeing my father again, I was never validated by him. It was kind of inevitable, really, that I would grow up to have a low value of myself. Recognizing how my growing-up years had impacted me was one of the keys to allowing myself to acknowledge how I had attracted the wrong men into my life, which led me to being able to (a) take responsibility and make necessary changes, and (b) forgive myself for having made the wrong choices and understand that I'd made the best choices I could given the skill set I'd had at the time.

I also acknowledged that giving consent to people to treat me badly wasn't a conscious decision, but an unconscious act based on my inner beliefs about myself. I saw that at the age of thirty-one I was at a junction in my life. I could choose to continue along the path well trodden, which, whilst familiar, wasn't serving me, or I could choose to take an untrodden path and explore who I might become along the journey. With a quote from Albert Einstein in my head—"Insanity is doing the same thing over and over again, expecting a different result"—I decided to take a deep breath and take the untrodden and unfamiliar path. If I wanted different results in all my relationships and life experiences, I would have to start thinking about myself in a different way. It wasn't easy—in fact, it was exceptionally painful at times. However, the light at the end of the tunnel was worth the darkness I had to brave to get there.

To start this inner change, I had to be really honest with myself, which, whilst not an easy thing to do, is incredibly empowering. I thought about ownership. The truth is, of course, that we actually own absolutely nothing in life. By that, I mean we don't own our homes (we either rent or have a mortgage); we don't own our cars; we don't own our clothes; we don't even own the money that we have in our purses, our bags, or our wallets. The reality is we simply have *temporary custody* of "things." A lot of what we think we "own" will still be here a long time after we have left this planet. We are custodians, pure and simple. Once I had accepted that fact, I realized the only thing I *actually* own are my thoughts. These are the very things no one can take away from me. Therefore, I am safe, now and for always, because I can't lose anything precious or of value. No one can derail me, unbalance me, bully me, or intimidate me. Once I had chosen to take full ownership and responsibility for my inner thoughts about myself and about other people, I was empowered to step into my feminine power. It's like having a bubble of protection around my aura; no one can penetrate this bubble, and within it I am safe and protected.

No matter what else is going on in my life at any given time, nobody can take my thoughts and my beliefs away from me. So, in fact, *I own everything I need to own.* This recognition allowed me to see how much power I had and how I was able to create my current reality and therefore my future. I moved from a position of feeling powerless, and allowing intimidation and low self-esteem to dictate my life, to a position of firmly rooted feminine power where I was able to step into my life fully and without personal censor.

How I Define Power

I would define the word "power" as being true to who you are every day. It is about knowing your values and living them every day through your actions, your thoughts, and your decisions.

Today I am very clear on my values and what I represent as a woman in the world. By being clear and true to who I am and my values, I am living authentically and on purpose. Being really true to myself allows me to take center stage, where I stand, firm and rooted, in a spotlight of assertiveness. There, I am able to ensure all my interactions are balanced and respectful. Assertiveness isn't about getting your own way no matter what—that's just aggressive behavior. Assertiveness is about showing respect for yourself and other people; it's the ability to create a win-win situation.

When women are truly powerful, they are able to step into their own spotlights and shine. For some women, this can feel "wrong," and feelings of self-consciousness and embarrassment can take over. Generally speaking, we are not brought up to take the spotlight. However, the mark of a powerful woman is being able to do this effortlessly, own her magnificence, and truly shine. If women can do this without the merest hint of any personal guilt or embarrassment, they will empower other women to do the same. One of my other favorite quotes is by Marianne Williamson from her poem, "Our Deepest Fear": "As we allow our own light to shine, we instinctively give others permission to do the same."

What Makes a Woman Powerful

Over the years I've worked with women, I've come to realize that so many people are unaware of what their personal values are. It isn't something we sit down and think about unless we make the concerted effort to do so. So how *do* you get to know what your values are? One way can be to take yourself back to when you were a teenager or young adult. Think about the things that gave you joy and made your heart sing, and also think about the things that made you angry. For example, when I was a teenager in the 1970s in London, England, there were a lot of national front riots happening about racism. This injustice absolutely incensed me. I was so furious that I wanted to attend a rally against the people who were being racist. Clearly fairness and justice were part of my set of values, even then. So it was no surprise that I ended up working in the field of diversity.

Give yourself some space in your day to sit down and think about what makes your heart sing and your soul light up, and also think about what makes you really, really angry. Don't be too "conscious" with this process—allow your unconscious to bubble up with what you write down. This is a great way to get in touch with your values and to embrace your feminine power. Through this process, we are allowing ourselves to connect to the strong core running through the universe and firmly linking us to the earth. From that very grounded center, we can then explore our uniqueness as women, for every one of us is different and special. Once we become firmly grounded and know that we are living our values every day, we can feel free to explore how we want to manifest our unique femininity in the world.

Tools for Connecting to Your Feminine Power

First of all, don't be a martyr! Did you know that stress has overtaken cancer and heart disease as the biggest killer of adults in the western world? Part of that stress is caused by living inauthentically. For women, this can mean living lives to suit those around us rather than living lives to suit ourselves. Women have a tendency to fall into the trap of losing the essence of who they are by attaching themselves to a label—like, for instance, "wife," "mother," "homemaker," or "daughter."

I don't think I've yet met a woman who doesn't put everybody else above herself. It's in our DNA; it's part of our makeup. I frequently challenge women by saying they are being incredibly selfish by putting everybody else first. They look at me completely aghast because the natural assumption is that they are being the opposite of that. However, constantly putting other people before yourself turns you into a martyr, and martyrs don't save anyone.

I use the analogy of the oxygen mask: When you are on a plane, the cabin crew members recite the safety procedures, saying, "If the plane loses pressure, an oxygen mask will fall down from the panel above you. Before helping those around you, make sure you attach your own mask first." Well, they say that for a reason. If we don't look after ourselves first, we are in no fit state to help anyone else. So making sure your energy levels are topped up and overflowing—and that you have looked after yourself with love, compassion and care—ensures you are acting *selflessly*, as people will always get the best of you, which you will give unconditionally and with love.

It is easy to fall into the trap, and get addicted to, the habit of being the martyr. Doing so then becomes a woman's identity. This goes back to my previous point. If you know your values and live by them, then you know who you are. If you know who you are, you are able to take good care of *you*, allowing you to step out of the martyr role and into one of empowerment.

In addition to being willing to give up martyrdom, giving up control—especially over other people—is another tool to connecting to your feminine power. Though many women would not want admit it, a lot of us do have a strong need to control. I think this probably comes from our motherly instincts, regardless of whether we become mothers. I am not a mother, but I witnessed how difficult it was for my own mother to let go of her control of me, especially as I was an only child. If we want to empower the next generation of women to be the best that they can be, though, we actually have to take our hands off, allow them to grow and develop, and let them make their own mistakes. We need to celebrate those mistakes, as it is only by making them that any of us can grow.

Potential problems can also arise when we try to control men! Men don't need or want to be controlled, nor do they want to be mothered. I recognize that at times in the past I attempted to do both—often at the same time!

I don't think of this trait in women as a weakness, but instead as a quality that is temporarily out of balance. This ability we have to take charge when necessary, organize everything and everyone, and care for the well-being of those around us is a wonderful quality—*if* we can keep it in balance. The problems start when we become controlling and smothering, or, on the other extreme, become uncaring and offer no boundaries whatsoever. The key to everything in life is balance. By stepping into, and owning, my feminine power, I was sure to nurture and care for myself first before offering this quality to others. I was also able to *offer* rather than *overwhelm* others, and I learnt not to be upset if my nurturing and/or organizational skills were not required. I am now able to care for those I love in a balanced and empowering way, enabling them to embrace their own power rather than become reliant on me.

Our New Role as Women and Our Challenges

For me, part of the new role for women is about celebrating masculinity! OK, I admit this may sound wrong in the context of this book and its message. However, I believe that it is only when we celebrate men for being who they are—men—that we are truly able to celebrate ourselves. I'll use the analogy of money. A lot of people feel resentful of others who have financial abundance. Going through life with this energy is self-destructive, as doing so gives the message to the universe that they view money, and the people who have it, as negative. Therefore they are keeping themselves in a *poverty mindset*. If women exude negative energy towards men with feelings of resentment, fear, anger and frustration, these women are keeping themselves in a *feminine-negative mindset*. In order to receive respect and celebration from others, we first have to give it. As I mentioned earlier, everyone has the ability to be her own mirror. The women who give out negativity towards men are disrespecting the masculine energy within themselves. We all have masculine and feminine energy, so the new role for women is to ensure this is in balance within ourselves, thus allowing men, too, to find their masculine and feminine balance.

Once we fully own with pride our feminine personalities and the wonderful qualities that accompany those personalities, we are able to "get out of our own way" and create a clear path for ourselves and the women coming up behind us. Which brings me to another point about the new role of women. I feel, very strongly, that it is my responsibility to honor and respect all the women who have gone before me, whether or not they are part of my bloodline. These women are the ones who did the real hard work; I have it easy in comparison. The choices I make about my life without a second thought are options that simply were not even on the radar for my mother, let alone her mother. The way I honor and respect all the powerful women who have lived before me is by embracing my authentic feminine power. If I were to mimic men, I would not only be disrespecting myself and disrespecting men, but worst of all, I'd be disrespecting all my female ancestors, which to me is unforgiveable. I also have a responsibility to create a clear path for all the fabulous women coming up behind me. I need to get it right.

Yes, women in the 21st century will face challenges as we fully embrace our femininity, but I prefer to view them as opportunities rather than challenges. If you are a woman in the Western World, you are currently living in the most privileged time in history. All of us have the opportunities and choices that our female ancestors could only dream about. This may sound harsh, but we need to get out of our own way and fully embrace this abundant, positive, and fruitful time in history.

We are lucky to live in a time when we can *value* our femininity. Back in the UK in the early 1980s, when women were just starting to enter very male-dominated industries and sectors, a culture of ball-breaking women emerged. We had our first woman Prime Minister in Margaret Thatcher, and other women were breaking into law, stock broking and finance. However, it was also a very shallow and materialistic period with very little spirituality. The key driver for people then was about how much money they could earn and how much champagne they could drink. It was also the time when women started to mimic every bad personality trait of men in business, and none of the good traits. This mimicking then became a habit—and habits, once formed, become entrenched in a person's behavior and become increasingly difficult to break. I feel as though women have been trying to break this habit for the last thirty years.

The moment I started stepping into my own feminine power with love and compassion, people around me, especially men, picked up on it unconsciously. I no longer invite negative relationships into my life because I don't need to. I've learnt the lessons I needed to learn, I've healed the inner part of me that made those decisions and I have forgiven myself, knowing it was all part of this amazing human experience that I have chosen to have right now! The older I get, the younger I become! I have more energy and vibrancy as a woman in my fifties than I did when I was a woman in my twenties. The pressures and angst I was carrying around when I was a young woman have gone. The liberated and free spirit that emerged from the mire is dancing with joy and delight! The older we get, the easier it is to meet ourselves exactly where we are.

As women, we can be our own worst enemies, and we have an amazing ability to hinder the changes that need to happen. We can't allow this. We must be able to consciously understand and accept ourselves in order for change to occur. Gandhi once said, "Be the change you want to see in the world." I am saying to you, "Be the change you want to see within yourself."

We must believe in our magnificence, and we must make a pact with ourselves to be the very best versions of who we are every single day, without censure, judgment, or embarrassment. We need to stand firmly rooted in the center of our feminine power, own that power without dilution, and from that core of strength know that we can change ourselves and the world around us. If we want to change the reflection when we look into the world mirror, we need to change the energy we put into the glass.

The decision I made to fully step into my feminine power was the best choice I could have made. When I look at myself in the mirror every morning, I really like the woman who is looking back at me. I respect her and I admire her, and I know that without the experiences that I have had, I would be someone different. I do, however, have certain regrets. I regret the time it took me to truly believe in myself and raise my level of self-esteem.

Every woman on the planet needs to recognize that she is unique and special. Think back to the very moment of your conception. OK, I know you can't because you didn't actually exist at the time! However, you can *imagine* it. Millions of sperm traveled up to try to impregnate the egg, and only one of them made it. All the others fell by the wayside and disappeared. The one that made it was the strongest, most resilient, unique, special, powerful and amazing. Part of that is you; that's what created you. So, if you doubt for a nanosecond that you are unique, special, and powerful, just think back to that point of conception. That power, strength, uniqueness, and brilliance was instantly part of you then, and it is still a part of you now. Take that seed of thought and nurture it. Every day it will grow and get stronger and more resilient.

Think of coming out of the season of winter and into spring. Whenever I see the bluebells, snowdrops, and crocuses burst forth from rock-hard ground, I think of their determination. These tiny, delicate flowers are so determined that they are going to have life and shine their brilliance on the world that nothing, not even concrete-hard mud, is going to stop them. So, think of yourself as a beautiful snowdrop, determined to shine your brilliance on the rest of the world!

CHAPTER 4

Kate Neligan

Kate Neligan is a Life and Career Coach & Founder of Synergy TV. Her coaching company, Conscious Rockstar, empowers women and men to create lives that rock. Kate's specialty is working with corporate groups and individuals in equine coaching; where she partners with horses that operate like mirrors to help people grow in self-awareness. Together, they teach and train people to develop effective communication and leadership skills that lead to success in all areas of life.

Kate also has a passion for sharing transformational and uplifting stories which she does through her mindful media company Synergy TV® (www.synergytvnetwork.com). She has curated hundreds of awe-inspiring short videos that mirror a better a world. Previously, Kate was the Vice President of Digital Marketing at Lionsgate where she promoted thousands of films and created successful partnerships with iTunes, Comcast, DIRECTV, Xbox and many more.

Kate holds a Master's degree in Spiritual Psychology from USM and her personal story on trailblazing can be found in the book "Women Will Save the World." Kate is a Huffington Post blogger and a motivational speaker with a TEDx talk entitled "The Pursuit of Perfection." Learn more at www.consciousrockstar.com.

My Story and My Journey to Power

My story is somewhat typical of anyone following the promise of the good old American Dream. I got good grades, went to a great college, worked hard to climb the corporate ladder, and earned many accolades for my hard work. I was Vice President of a movie studio at the early age of thirty-one, and with the position came a secure, sizable paycheck but also a big itch. I had somehow bought into someone else's plan for my life. Maybe it was my parents or society or just my own ego's need for control, safety, security, glamour, and recognition, but I felt like my soul was shriveling and no matter what, I couldn't reach the spot that itched.

To many, I was in a position of power. I had a staff, made a lot of big decisions, and was regarded as an expert in my field, participating in industry events and panels. While I did have a decent amount of external power, something was still missing. I came to realize I was craving inner power and my own feminine nature. I was searching for my heart and for ways to be of service to something outside of my "inner driver" that kept me chasing the next goal, always in pursuit of happiness but never really fulfilled.

Like many of us, I thought it was important to have a good title and large salary, and work toward a nice house, car, and family. There is nothing wrong with wanting any of these things if our intentions are clean, but I was placing value on everything that was external. Each time I achieved something, I still felt an emptiness that left me frustrated. I thought if I could just get to the next magical goal (or scratch the itch for good!), I would feel good enough. Many of my choices were driven by wanting people to like me. It is so clear to me now that I was giving my power away. I was letting societal norms define my life path. I was making other people's opinions of me more important than my own.

My goal-centered, ego-centered life was obviously not working for me, so I knew I needed to shift. I started to understand that people's beliefs about me and who I was were none of my business and they were outside of my control. During this time, I got my Master's Degree in Spiritual Psychology from the University of Santa Monica and I did a lot of deep, inner work about my own irrational beliefs and patterns of behavior. I started to clean up my intentions, cultivate the heart-centered feminine virtues, and develop strategies to effectively move through issues quickly. I started to see and believe in myself as a divine being having a human experience, not just a human being who occasionally felt divine.

Around this time, I also started to feel a huge pull to be of service, and I began to share my gifts in a way that helped the world. I loved media, but I wanted to use it for good and to inspire and uplift the world. I wanted to promote mindful, healing, transformative and conscious content, so I founded a curated video channel that synergizes personal development and entertainment called Synergy TV (*www.synergytvnetwork.com*). This made me happy, and it was something I had power over— my own choices. This process of getting to know the real me and then sharing myself as a loving force in the world made me feel powerful beyond measure, and I became itch-free! So my journey has been like that of the butterfly, transforming from a creepy crawler with limited sight to a beautiful, winged-creature that can soar and create smiles wherever I go because I am guided by my own light.

How I Define Power

Yogi Bhajan said, "To be a woman is the last, highest incarnation." Living the truth of whom and what we are—divine beings having human experiences—is what really makes us powerful. I define true power as the expression of our authentic loving self that fulfills us and magnetizes great experiences to us. Sometimes we forget that we are women, and we become a chameleon to whatever role we think is required of us in the moment (i.e., mother, daughter, wife, friend, co-worker). In corporate America, that might even be acting like men to succeed or fit in. In order to embrace our feminine power, however, we need to embrace and own our feminine characteristics, traits, and energy.

What Makes a Woman Powerful

At one point in my career, I realized I was trying to be the best man I knew how to be because all of my role models were men. I didn't know any strong female leaders, so I emulated the men I worked for, which over time left me with adrenal burn-out, irritability, and a feeling like I had lost myself. The notion that we have to work really hard, strive, and take massive action is a mentality that a lot of us have grown up with in America, and it's actually a very masculine way of being. I was so misguided, thinking that I needed to be like a man in order to succeed and to grow. When I realized that I was making a mistake in disowning my natural power center, I started to ask questions and I found the answers inside.

My higher Self and intuition guided me to embrace more of my feminine characteristics, and I began to live from my own truth as a woman. While I love to get things done and take action, I also value states of being which include playfulness, vulnerability, gentleness, calmness, quietness, and connectedness. I believe power is really about authentic truth, integrity, and alignment. It is when we embrace our true nature, own our inherent gifts and qualities, and share them with the world that our lives start to take off and we feel more alive and more effective at life.

Women are special creatures. It's in our nature to be caretakers, yet we want to be taken care of, too. We want to be appreciated not just for our minds and bodies, but also for our inner lights. We are, as men have told us for ages, complex. Often, we seem to want two entirely different things at once or we send out mixed signals. We want to be strong and yet we yearn for softness and gentleness. We want to be powerful and yet we give our power away frequently. We want to feel sexy and yet we don't want to be thought of as sex symbols. Sometimes we come across as walking contradictions. I believe this is because we have become confused about our true nature and our real source of power.

In all the masks we wear, the biggest disservice we can do to ourselves is to abandon our femininity and act like a man. From experience, I can tell you this simply won't work. We are at a tipping point in society where a resurgence of the feminine heart-centered virtues of compassion, nurturing, intuition, receptivity, and synergy are coming back. These qualities are our true nature and our power centers as women. If we choose to embrace them, we will help our Planet course-correct, and together we can change the world for the better.

Tools for Connecting to Your Feminine Power

It is so easy to get caught up in the trap of associating power with material things or external experiences, but when we get quiet, go within, slow down, and access and ignite the true source of our natural flowing power, it always comes from our higher Self. I call this our "Conscious Rockstar™" and this inner experience shows up as a voice, feeling, or knowing that guides us to greatness. She is your best friend, your biggest fan, your wise sage, and your source of unconditional love. Being in touch with her on a daily basis and allowing her to lead your life is what it takes to be an empowered woman in today's world.

A woman's power and Conscious Rockstar™ is activated when she is in tune with her highest potential. Once evoked, this essence of being is a deep core of truth that is unshakeable and full of purpose. She then works as a magnet does and pulls things to you in a way where you have to work less and are open to receiving more. To cultivate true inner power and rockstar-essence, women need to focus on five of their natural abilities, which are to be nurturing, receptive, compassionate, intuitive, and synergized. I have created a list of tips and tools on how to connect with and stay centered in your feminine power (and access your Conscious Rockstar™) on my website at *www.consciousrockstar.com*. Here are five ways you can start right now.

#1 Nurturing

Women are both trained and coded to be caregivers. This is why you see many nursing, educational, service-oriented fields filled with women. As we raise children and care for friends and spouses, we learn how to value others. As entrepreneurs, we learn how to grow our businesses. This natural ability also makes us great stewards of the environment. More and more women are making conscious purchasing choices around food, cleaning products, cars, and clothes. We have much to teach the world about how we can care for each other. We also have much to learn about how we can care for ourselves first. In every airplane, we are told to put our oxygen mask on first—and so we must also put our health and vitality before those we love. Only then can our nurturing cups be full enough to overflow, so we don't get depleted, frustrated, and resentful. We can't be powerful when we are tired, grumpy, hungry, numb, or emotionally stuffed up. Many women have taken on more than is expected of them simply because they can, but it doesn't mean they should.

I believe that it is time for all women to start to make their own lives their #1 priority. You may be a single mom with literally no time, but just a few minutes a day can make a world of difference for your own sanity and the happiness of those around you. Remember you can't "find time," but you can create it. We all have the same amount of hours in a day, but the best thing you can do for yourself is to nurture your soul, your heart, and your inner child. My suggestion is to start with a minimum of ten minutes for yourself in the morning and ten minutes for yourself in the evening. Ask your Conscious Rockstar™ for the best ways that you can nurture yourself, and write them down and schedule them in your planner. Here is an affirmation that you can say each day to remind you to focus on you: *"I'm taking care of myself first so I can also take care of others."*

#2 Receptive

One thing that has always fascinated me is watching women in power who are able to do less and receive more. They have learned the "art of allowance." Women are physically designed to receive; that is how we are biologically shaped. Giving is certainly one of our strengths, yet many of us give so much that we don't know how to receive. Sometimes we feel so overwhelmed and burned out from being caretakers that we are depleted of our own energy. This is one of the challenges of the modern woman because it is not a sustainable way of living. We need to create systems that are sustainable on the individual level and the global level so that our society will not only survive but will thrive as well. The good news is there is always unending love and energy that you can tap at any time. Your Conscious Rockstar™ is your access point, and she is in a constant connection with this positive energy and flow. If you connect with that and allow yourself to be filled with this light and love, you can give from that place. This is your receiving dock, and through receptive energy you can actually accomplish more. It is similar to how you plug your phone into the wall to receive the electricity to recharge or it won't work.

Another challenge we face as women is the expectation that we have to do it all—and do it ourselves. That is an old paradigm and it's not true. It's simply your ego's wish to struggle. When we receive help, we can actually do a lot more. Think of the archetype of the Queen. She allows others to serve her, and her homeland still runs with efficiency. She is often portrayed as confident and in charge. My suggestion is to look for situations and experiences where you feel an even cycle of giving and receiving. (This is when you can't tell the difference between what you are giving and receiving because both feel abundant and good.) Those are the healthy situations, relationships, projects, and jobs that will keep you in balance. For me, whenever I am with clients in the arena as an equine coach, I feel the balanced flow as I give my time, love, compassion, expertise, and coaching and I receive the beauty of my clients' vulnerability, the power of their transformation, and the blessing of their financial investment. You can start this cycle by saying YES the next time someone asks you, "Would you like help with that?" Let a store clerk carry your bags, and give him a smile. Be grateful and receive like a Queen. It is this ability to receive that actually brings us everything that we truly desire. An affirmation you can work with is: *"I receive like a Queen as I plug in my receiving dock each day to recharge."*

#3 Compassionate

Right now the world needs a whole lot more compassion. People are suffering everywhere we look, it seems, but a woman's loving, compassionate nature can shine a light in even the darkest places. Compassion is a way of being, and it's natural to many women. Maybe it comes from our motherly tendencies or listening to men and their struggles for so many centuries, but it's something we just do well. My definition of compassion is being centered in our hearts and fully present with another while we are fully present with ourselves. This means we can take care of our own needs and emotions while simultaneously taking care of someone else's. It's the only form of multitasking that I know works wonders. Men love to fix things, and they often see problems and go after them in an effort to solve them. Women, on the other hand, can approach the world as though it's not broken at all. They know that their deep listening and holding space for someone to emote and vent can be healing. This is what we need to do as a collective right now. Each woman needs to commit to a practice of compassion and offer this loving space to her family, friends, and the world. Men will follow as we lead by example, and they feel the benefits.

A compassion practice can be completed with just five minutes every day in a peace meditation. Pick at least one specific time each day (I like noon) and close your eyes and think of an animal or friend or family member you love the most. Get in touch with this love and then fill your entire being with it and then radiate it outwards to your personal circles (i.e., work, family, friends) and then to the world. Send it to all places where you know there is conflict, and picture that area flooded with pink light. At times, you will go through challenges and need your own compassion as well. This is when you call on your Conscious Rockstar™ and ask her for compassionate advice. She will tell you, "It's going to be okay," "This, too, shall pass," "You didn't do anything wrong," and "I love you no matter what." Let her loving voice clear out any frustration or fear or sadness you might feel at the time. You can also put your hand on your heart and forgive yourself and others for anything that might be upsetting you. Compassion dissolves lower vibrations and difficult feelings that keep you stuck. If every government in the world started to practice this, we would no longer have wars. Imagine the world we could live in with more compassion. An affirmation you might use is: *I am a loving, compassionate being capable of giving and receiving unconditional love.*

#4 Intuitive

Women need to listen to the wise sage inside, their inner rockstar, which empowers them to do amazing things in the world. To me, the word "rockstar" describes someone who's living on purpose, shining his or her light, and being fully alive. Being a Conscious Rockstar™ is really about being awake and aware by taking the highest and best path in our lives. In order to live lives that rock, women need to be aware that the helpful voice in their heads, their intuition, is what makes them feel like rockstars. For some people, it may take time to connect to this part. The key is to be really patient with this inner compass and to spend time every day connecting with that voice and asking her questions, like you would ask a trusted advisor. Ask questions like: "What would you have me do today?" "What's for my highest good?" "How can I be of service?" "What are my gifts?" and "Why am I here?" You will receive answers. It's a matter of really slowing down and setting a strong intention to connect with that voice and then being patient and listening to any signs or words or pictures that show up to help guide you.

When you really listen to your inner voice and begin to understand that you are a Conscious Rockstar™, you will understand what your calling is and how to follow it. I thought my calling was to run a movie studio, but that was more about my ego's desire for status and worldly success. I now define success as doing what I love. What I love to do is inspire and help others, and I do this in many ways that all work for me and those I serve. We all have to go through a lot of conscious listening to be mindful of the signs, the symbolism, and synchronicities in our life to really see where we're being guided. I believe we're always being guided to share our gifts, which is why I love helping women (and men too!) step into knowing what they're here for and how to take steps forward in the direction of their dreams. Each morning you can write out a question to your Conscious Rockstar™ or intend to connect with her in meditation. Then all you need to do is quiet your mind and stay open. An affirmation you can use is: *"I am always connected to my inner wisdom and light, and I receive helpful guidance all the time."*

#5 Synergized

To become synergized means to step into wholeness. You are already a whole complete being, but if you believe you need to be someone other than you are, you are wearing a mask. If you believe you are broken in any way, you aren't in synergy. The definition of synergy is that the whole is greater than the sum of its parts. To me, this is a miraculous mathematical equation that includes your higher Self. All of the roles you play do not make you whole, but add in your connection to something greater than you (a.k.a., your Conscious Rockstar™), and you are whole! States of synergy are like states of balance, and they can't be forced. Synergy comes from setting an intention to see yourself as connected to all things. In this interconnected worldview, you can see how you play a small but necessary part. This keeps you both humble and empowered, which is a beautiful way to be in the world.

Women are most powerful when we balance our masculine and feminine energies and synergize the benefits of both. The key is to know when each energy is needed, based on the situation you are in and the role you are playing. As wife and mother, you may need a lot more feminine energy, but if you need to accomplish various errands or tasks quickly, you may need to switch into masculine energy. To stand up for yourself, be assertive, draw boundaries, and ask for promotions, you may need to embrace the benefits of masculinity. Men naturally know how to put themselves first and go after what they want. This is why a lot of men have worldly power—because they understand what it means to honor their needs. As women, we need to be unapologetic about receiving what we need in order to shine. To practice synergy, all you need to do is set the intention to feel connected to all beings and all parts of yourself. Check in before you do a task, and ask yourself if you need more feminine or masculine energy. Then you can switch back and forth as easily as a light switch as you cultivate this skill. An affirmation you can work with is: *"I am synergized, whole, and complete as I play with my masculine and feminine energy."*

Our New Role as Women and Our Challenges

Once women really practice and embrace these natural abilities, they often step into larger leaderships roles. Women are actually a lot more influential than we give ourselves credit for. We simply need to stop hiding or giving away our power and start noticing how we already have all the power we would ever need to live a fulfilling life. We can't blame men for the power struggles we see. We have to take responsibility for our power. We are often the center of many men's lives, as they turn to us when they most need a friend or compassionate advice. We are their mothers and their sisters and teachers, often raising them and/or training them. Men will tell you that their favorite thing is to see us happy. Therefore, women need to lead by example! If we want the people around us to change, we have to change first, as we can only control our own state of being.

By being and sharing the five qualities mentioned above, men too can embrace these important feminine qualities that will help connect the world and move us out of a competitive culture and into an interconnected one. Before I was a female entrepreneur, I saw a lot of leadership that was based on power struggles— leaders needing to be in control and having the final word. I saw how this damaged teamwork and created resentment. I realized that true power is about synergistic threads of collaboration. The loving leader recognizes and appreciates the strengths and contributions of each team member. People feel more motivated and rewarded when they are acknowledged and honored by someone. Often we are so entrenched in this world of dog-eat-dog and rapid technological access that we don't take moments to slow down, breathe, and truly see and hear another human being. Men need us to love them and acknowledge them. And let's be honest, we need men, too, but we don't need to be them.

The role of women has changed over the years, and it is an exciting time because we are stepping into new roles. Now we can see ourselves as leaders, as influencers, and as the change-agents we wish to see in the world. My experience of myself and other women is that we're moving through issues a lot more quickly and we're stepping and aligning more with our own truths. As women, our role in this new paradigm is to embrace our feminine energy that brings us all back to our centers, to a sustainable lifestyle, and to nurturing all beings. It is time for all women to stand up for what we believe to be right and good and to speak our truths about who we are and why we appreciate our femininity. There are many women around the world without a voice, and those of us who are blessed to write in books like this one must take the time and responsibility to represent the whole by shining a light on what is needed for all women: a return to our loving essence, freedom, appreciation, and truth.

I encourage you to ignite your inner light and embrace your powerful feminine essence that is reawakening at this critical time in our shared history. What qualities are you currently rocking? Which ones do you need to cultivate more? If you are reading this, then you are being called to become even more of a spiritual warrior, cosmic mother, radiant goddess, Conscious Rockstar™, and empowered woman who positively influences the greater good! You are a radiant blessing to yourself, your loved ones, and the world.

CHAPTER 5

Sue Liburd

Sue Liburd is a multi award-winning businesswoman, author, organisational development consultant, keynote speaker and high performance executive coach. Working across multiple industry sectors and disciplines, Sue works around the globe in the Middle East, India, US, China and mainland Europe for large corporations. Widely recognised and endorsed for her expertise in organisational transformation, talent development and cultural change, she infuses this thinking and her practice with insights taken from trends within the changing human capital management and technology landscape.

Sue is particularly passionate about the enablement of leaders as they grapple with the changing notions of work and seek to create workplace cultures where both women and men desire to be. An emerging thought leader on the gender diversity imperative in business, she is influencing thinking at the highest levels. Website: http://www.sueliburd.com.

My Story and My Journey to Power

Rather than start with a career chronology, I'll begin with revealing two key ingredients of my secret sauce of being a woman who is attuned to her power.

At the heart of my personal power is a set of core beliefs, which include "Success is never complete" and "Each day we need to put ourselves to the test." As a consequence, I perceive my life as a daily adventure. I grew up reading a lot of Greek mythology, for example tales of Hera, Aphrodite, Jason and the Argonauts, Theseus and the Minotaur, and the adventures of Odysseus and the Trojan horse. At the core of all these stories are tales of individuals overcoming challenges and adversity. In addition, I listened to my parents' stories about the dreams and aspirations they had as children and the challenges of leaving the Caribbean to create a new life in England. I have inculcated into my life these rich stories of adventure and the hero's and heroine's quests; they have instilled in me a spirit of adventure and the ability to see this life as a journey.

I perceive myself today as being the sum total of all my adventures and a composite of the knowledge, skills, gifts, and talents that I have acquired along the way. I utilize these abilities as my superpower in service to others, whilst living a full and adventurous life. The word I use to describe myself is an Italian term, CONSIGLIERE. Consigliere means wise counselor, trusted advisor, a person acting as a personal strategist to decision makers. To be deemed Consigliere, you have to have a broad depth of experience.

Because I have a range of personae, I have amassed a vast repository of experiences that I draw upon as Consigliere. Today my career portfolio includes the roles of author, speaker, change and transformation consultant, and executive coach. Working globally, I have the opportunity to meet and work with many different people, interact with many cultures, and experience differing ways of seeing the world. In addition, I am the founder and managing director of several companies, as well as being a non-executive director on a range of boards for other companies.

Seeking to live a life rich in experience and learning whilst being in service to others is at the heart of what I do. I focus my time and energy on helping individuals and organizations to change and transform their thinking and behavior to achieve something better than they have today. My career and personal life embodies that.

I started my professional life in nursing and midwifery, originally training and qualifying as a Registered General Nurse (RGN), Registered Mental Nurse (RMN) and Registered Midwife (RM), working in the National Health Service (NHS) where healthcare is provided free of charge at the point of entry for UK citizens. During this chapter in my life I worked with and experienced people from all strata of society. When people walk through a hospital door, they are in an environment that is unfamiliar, and they often feel vulnerable and uncertain. One of the key things I learnt was how to deal with people who are experiencing concern, doubt, anxiety, and fear and are in a vulnerable emotional state. Because of those formative experiences, when I work with clients today in large, complex, fast-paced organizations and corporations going through change and transformation, I am well equipped to recognize and manage feelings of vulnerability, uncertainty, and sometimes fear.

I made the move out of the NHS because life and events started to feel repetitive and predictable. Concerned that if I stayed, my dreams and ambitions wouldn't materialize, and fearing the next thirty to forty years would be uneventful, I knew it was time for a change. I had a vision of a lifestyle that included new challenges and opportunities to travel and meet a diverse range of interesting people. So I looked to the Armed Forces. It's not as strange a career choice as it quite sounds! I come from a military background—my father had served in the Royal Air Force, and my brother was in the Royal Navy—so the Armed Forces wasn't a completely alien concept for me.

I joined the British Army for several reasons, most notably because there was a perceived glass ceiling for women, and as a black woman, there were going to be even more levels of difficulty. As I love a challenge, I said, "You know what? I'm going to dance on that glass ceiling, have an amazing experience, travel the world, meet new people, and get a basket full of different experiences and new skills." And that's exactly what happened. I served as an army officer for seven years and I left holding the rank of Captain, taking with me good memories, a clutch of new skills, great experiences, and some good friends.

Upon leaving the army, I worked in the charitable sector, at the national headquarters of the British Red Cross. From there I went into social housing and community development. With a desire to one day own my own business, I moved into the commercial corporate and consultancy arena before setting out on the journey of the entrepreneur. As part of the journey, I continued my formal and informal education, graduating with multiple degrees, diplomas, and certificates. The journeys and experiences that I've had along the way, and the people's lives that I've touched and

How I Define Power

I believe power is like the pure properties of water—natural, soft, fluid, and flexible. You can't grab hold of water and hang on to it with your hands. If you try to change its basic nature, it becomes something else. When it freezes, it's no longer water; it has become ice. You heat it up, it's no longer water; it has become steam. Doctor Masaru Emoto, author and scientific researcher on the molecular properties of water, demonstrated how water is "aware" and has the ability to reflect the consciousness of its environment. For example, in his experiments, he observed that when you paste a written note of gratitude, love, or happiness to a bottle containing water, it will create beautiful patterned crystals when frozen. Conversely, if you attach unpleasant or negative messages, malformed, incomplete, or unpleasant crystals are formed on freezing. Water is a blueprint for personal power. Ever present, it has the ability to sustain life; however, it also has the potential to do immense harm.

When I stand in my personal power, fear, doubt and anxiety do not exist and I have full access to all my internal personal resources and my authentic self. I am confident, energizing, and able to influence without control, adopting a gentle focus with purpose. I am conscious, present, fluid and nurturing in my approach. Not attached to the good opinion of others or their dogma, I choose to use my personal power to positively disrupt, change, and influence people and organizations—always aware that when something is out of flow, there is potential to do harm.

Like water that yesterday was running from a stream into a river and is now heading towards the ocean, adapting and evolving through its daily encounters with its environment, my basic nature remains the same whilst I evolve and develop as I flow from where I am now to where I plan to be.

What Makes a Woman Powerful?

Women are very powerful, but so many women don't realize it. Our sphere of influence is intergenerational. What makes us powerful is our multiple skills and talents—plus, the world cannot survive without us. How powerful is that? The world! Not just one or two individuals, but the world! We make up half of the world's population now. That, to me, is both powerful and significant.

Another beautiful thing about women is we've got both a feminine and masculine aspect. I believe power for women comes when we embrace both the masculine and the feminine aspects of ourselves. If necessary, we can fight and protect, but we can also heal, collaborate, and nurture in equal measure. Because of our feminine and masculine aspects, we have freedoms today in this part of the world that have been hard won for us; this now resides in our collective DNA. We've got a repository of experiences that all women can call upon whenever we need it—we just have to tap into that collective. So what makes us powerful? We're just an amazing species on this planet. We are women.

Tools for Connecting to Your Feminine Power

Connecting with my feminine power has been an integral part of my journey. First of all, I learned to redefine success based on who I am, my talents, my gifts, and a belief that life is an adventure. I have to thank my dad for that. One of the things he said to me when I was growing up was, "Sue, when people first see you, they're going to see your color first. They're not going to see 'you' and who you are. They're not going to see your talents, your gifts, everything that you bring to this world. They're going to see color first, and then they'll see your gender."

Living and working in a society that was made up of the constructs of the white male, I needed to reconsider the criteria for my success. I'm not anti white men—please don't think that—but I live in a part of the world where the construct is based on the needs and views of the white male. For example, when, over the last fifty years, we talked about leadership, strength, or success, a lot of the language used was—and continues to be—male-dominated. I recognized that being black and being a woman, there was something that I needed to do: redefine what I perceived success to be. In redefining success, I've been able to connect with my own feminine power.

Secondly, I started to ask myself simple but powerful transformational questions. For example, "Who gave me that opinion?" It is still a question I ask myself today. If I hold a view about something or find myself talking about something in a particular way, I'll ask, "Where did that opinion come from? Was that something that I just picked up in the media? Have I synthesized a range of information and drawn that conclusion or created that opinion myself?"

Growing up, I would ask myself, "What would I do if it was me in that situation, and why?" My mum was great at helping me make sense of some of this thinking. This helped me start to think about who I wanted to be, what actions was I going to take in order to achieve a particular desired result, and what opinions was I choosing to believe.

The third ingredient was one of curiosity. Just being curious and not living on autopilot helped me to recognize that I could change or shape things if I wished. This belief, apart from being highly liberating, has helped me navigate my ups and downs as I benchmark myself against my standards of achievement and my own notions of success—not those determined by someone else. Doing that has made me far stronger and resilient and therefore able to stand firmly in my own power, fulfilling a script I design for myself and not living a life based on a set of rules dictated by somebody else.

Below are my tips and tools for other women to connect with their feminine power.

Tip number 1: redefine your success. Success needs to be measured on our terms, not somebody else's image of success. Create a personal definition of success, or in any given moment ask yourself, "What does success look like for me?" I think it's a key question that as women we should regularly be asking ourselves. Success doesn't need to be what society tells us. When I say society, I mean the media or male-dominated constructs. Once again, I want to emphasize that I'm not anti-men. I love men. I cannot imagine our world without them, nor would I want to, but the male version of success is not the only version of success.

Tip number 2: embrace change and take action. Do something differently every day and become comfortable with change. We can't stand still; the world around us is changing rapidly. Like death and taxes, change is a constant in modern day living. How we live life is changing, and therefore, as women, one of the key things for our future success is to keep moving forward, even if it's just taking a small step at a time.

Tip number 3: find and commit to a purpose, whatever that purpose might be. No matter if it changes over a period of time, I encourage you to find it, commit to it, and start moving toward it. This will give meaning to everything you do. Whether you are a mother, a care provider, someone career focused, or someone whose purpose is growing flowers and having an amazing garden, find whatever "it" is and commit to a purpose.

My fourth tip is a big one: I encourage all women to remember that if at first you don't succeed, try again. Sometimes we wriggle with our doubt; we lack confidence, and we're hugely critical about ourselves. This life is an iterative journey—which means, in short, that you get a lot of chances to repeat things—and to even change how you do them. And it's about experimentation, so if you don't succeed at something, you get another go at it. Try a different way, and you'll discover that even when resources are limited, magic happens and dreams come true. I believe that.

My fifth tip is to embrace the different phases in our lives. We're not going to be teenagers forever, nor are we to be eternally in our twenties, thirties, forties or fifties, so we need to face up to this fact. Our bodies will change, our thinking will change, our attitude will change, and our loves and dislikes will change.

This tip is about embracing the different phases in our life on the journey to becoming a wise elder.

My sixth tip is to remember to take care of yourself. One strategy that works well for me is making dates with myself. We spend so much time as women giving to other people that we often don't give to ourselves. For many years, I have put ME DATES in the diary. I simply go on dates with myself; they are those scheduled moments when I get to totally treat myself. ME dates are about me valuing me. Whether it is a long soak in the bath, a walk in a park, the cinema for an afternoon matinee, a spa day, museum or gallery visit, I do these things on my own. A ME date is a time when I can step away from day to day activities and step off the "hamster wheel." The dates have been a great way for me to ground myself and remind me who I am, why I'm here, and what it is that I want from my life.

As women, we are the queens of multitasking. We do so much, so I entreat women who have made life choices where you can't put your needs first for the whole time that you're on the planet to at least a couple of times a month find some moments when you can make time for a ME Date.

Another important part of taking care of yourself is choosing not to live a life of regret—a topic I mentioned earlier. Sometimes we're so busy that we put our own hopes and dreams on the back burner and they get slowly extinguished. Don't get to a point where you're at end of this life, saying, "I wish I'd done. I wish I'd done." This life is about having experiences and adventures on the way; it's about living an experiential life. I'm clear about who I want to be in this life and what I want to achieve, and I'm like that river purposely moving towards the ocean. Sometimes the flow is very quick, and sometimes there's a whole heap of stuff on my plate and it feels very sluggish or slow, but I just know that I'm moving forward, meandering toward what it is that I want to do. So my advice to women is: wherever we are in our life on our journey, whatever stage of life we're in, keep it simple, have experiences, and have adventures—whilst being in service to others because that's kind of what we do as women.

Finally, tip number seven: some of the most difficult moments that we have in this life can lead to the most profound learning. We don't often recognize the gift until we get to other side. We just need to remember to harvest the learning from time to time so we don't get trapped in a cycle of repeated mistakes.

In summary, connect with your feminine power, which requires you to take action. And remember that it's OK to be more contentious, to fear less, to embrace change, and to redefine your success.

Our New Role as Women and Our Challenges

Though I'm not sure there's a new role, I do think there is a refining or tweaking that needs to take place, which is about women getting clear about who we are, what our talents and gifts are, and how we plan to use them while we're here in this lifetime in whatever roles we're undertaking. I know such refining is easier said than done, but in my experience when women get clear— when we get on purpose, when we are striving for something, whether that's to own our business, give kids the best start in life, or to be the most awesome partner on this planet—we are awesome.

I think our biggest challenge is that there is a fundamental disrespect of women in the world, and I believe that we as women collude with that. I live in a part of the world where we don't have equal pay for equal work; where women have equal access to education and are well educated, and yet that's not necessarily valued; where we're still battling to get our voices heard; and where a lot of derogatory language invariably disrespects women.

How do we overcome some of the challenges of being a woman? We accept that it's OK to be human, we don't have to be perfect, and we don't have to do it all. We can't be the super housekeeper, be an awesome parent, have an amazing professional career, be a supermodel, be the best lover, and be strong and confident all at once. The list is endless, and that can drown us. We don't expect this of men, so why do we expect this of ourselves? I think we should rewrite the script. One of the biggest challenges is for us to turn around and say, "I'm redefining my success, and I'm redefining what being a woman means for me." I also want to say to women, particularly women who have sons, please educate your boys because these are the husbands, brothers, uncles, and influencers of tomorrow.

I encourage women not to be complacent. The gains we have made in our society, in particular in this part of world, have been hard won and fought for. Women in other parts of the world aspire and dream of the freedom of choice and access to education that we have. So please do not to take it for granted, and do not become complacent about it.

Finally, I think one of best ways to overcome the challenges we face today as women is to see life as a daily adventure. When you see things as an adventure, as a personal quest where we are playing the role of heroine overcoming challenge and adversity in our personal story, it changes everything. Just remember to notice and celebrate the small wins. I've seen this simple but powerful philosophy work for women who were economically dependent upon physically abusive men as they eased their way out of destructive relationships, as well as high-flying corporate women struggling with their work/life balance and half-remembered dreams.

I know at times it can be difficult being a woman. I understand it, I have seen it, and I have journeyed alongside women who have been in extreme difficulty; however, when we find and tap into the essence of being a woman and our feminine power, we can change the world.

CHAPTER 6

Elizabeth Locey

Elizabeth Locey, Ph.D., is an Oracle who helps influencers and business leaders around the world turn up the volume on their competitive edge, with mind-blowing answers channeled straight from Source. In addition to impeccable soul-truth information, she specializes in healing self-sabotage. Formerly an award-winning professor of French Literature and Women's Studies, Elizabeth now teaches conscious entrepreneurs how to boost energy and income using fun tools like intuition and crystals. Check out the cool stuff she shares on her blog, www.elizabethlocey.com, and join the conversation.

My Story and My Journey to Power

At first blush, my story looks like it's all over the map. It's really not, though: we come full circle, *and* there are no lost steps.

As a little girl, I was very Piscean, really connected to the Universe. I must have been about four when I had what today I would call a powerful intuitive hit. I was looking up into the sky while holding onto a branch of flowering forsythia. All of a sudden I got it: "*Oh*, so *this* is the dream and *out there* is the reality." And I also knew that I wasn't going to be able to tell my parents or anyone else.

So, I just stayed to my little dreamy self. For my first few years of school, I was the classic space cadet. I was smart enough that I could get by without paying attention in class; I would just watch the sky all day. My parents were both professors, and in second or third grade, I realized that I could get approval from them by excelling in school. From that moment of realization until some thirty-five years later when I quit my job as a professor, I followed the path of intellect.

Or so I told myself. Actually, starting in my first year of college, I began to (re)connect powerfully with women's history. Women's spirituality and our role as leaders during the Goddess Age caught my attention and held it for years.

And so, even as I was focused on academics and was very successful in that realm, I was also filled with a thirst for knowledge of the Old Ways. I was indulging a taste for fantasy fiction and history rewritten from the women's perspectives (Marion Zimmer Bradley in particular) while maintaining a rigorous academic schedule.

In my "main life," it was dean's list, masters with honors, Ph.D., and then award-winning professor and internationally known scholar. In my "hidden life," I was opening up. After years of having shut myself away from these universal principles, I was connecting with them again.

During my graduate school years (I call them my seven-year sceptic's bootcamp), I was really starting to connect to nature, the moon, and my own power as a spiritual woman, though I never would have put it in those terms at the time. I discovered and was fascinated by things like Bach flower essences and kinesiology and was vaguely connected to the pagan community in town. But that was all just for fun—not something to be taken seriously. The closer I got to the doctorate, the less I was able to believe in anything that had not been scientifically proven.

My double life reached cruising altitude once I became a professor. There were three big turning points that brought me to leaving a career for which I'd been training my entire life.

The first turning point—it was more like a sea-change—occurred in my first year. I'd started seeing a therapist after a whirlwind love affair that had crash-landed. One of the first things she said to me was, "You're clearly not trusting the Universe." I didn't want to hear it. Through middle school I had been quite tuned in to God energies, but then the church and I had a serious falling out. At sixteen, I slammed that door as hard as I could, and fifteen years later, in her office, it started to pry itself back open, with me pushing hard against it all the way.

Three years into our client-therapist relationship, at the end of a session, she said, "I have something to tell you. It's become a really important part of my life, but I'm not sure how you're going to take it, so here goes: I've started channelling an entity named Michael, and he wants to say hi."

Hel-lo! I decided I would *not* roll my eyes or snort, as I was inclined to do—she was a dear, dear friend, after all. Instead, I decided to get out of there. I started to stand up from the sofa where I'd been sitting, but the "hi" from Michael was already underway.

I've never experienced anything more powerful in my entire life. It was like an *atomic bomb of Love* dropped into the room.

The blast field of that Love bomb threw me back into the sofa and pinned me there. It was crazy; my eyes were like saucers. "Whoa! What is that?" All of a sudden, my friend wasn't really my friend. It looked like her, and kind of sounded like her, but it *definitely wasn't her*. It was someone else doing a rapid-fire cosmic comedy routine of Divine Love with her body.

In an instant, I went from thinking "Channelling is something invented to manipulate woolly-minded people" to "Oh, my gosh! This stuff is real!"

It was as though gravity had ceased to exist for me. My whole world was turned upside down.

What I didn't anticipate on that day was that within a couple of months *I would be channelling an entity of my own.* His name was Georgie, and he had tusks, like a walrus. My Georgie period lasted for a couple of years, and I tried to hide it from everyone in my life. My sweetheart, a philosophy professor, left me when he found out: he still thought people who believed in channeling were woolly-minded, much as I had not so long before.

In my heartbreak, I closed that door marked "Divine Energies" again for years. I tried to settle down and be as "normal" as possible: I became chair of the department, got married, and was about to start a family.

The metaphysical world stepped back into my life radically as I was enjoying the end of my second trimester of pregnancy: this was turning point #2. What happened next cracked me wide open and set me on my current path.

I was six months pregnant, and out of nowhere, my daughter was about to be born. A massive flu was masking what we later learned was pre-eclampsia, and suddenly, two lives were on the line.

After a round of particularly cinematic projectile vomiting, the blood vessels in my brain started to swell, and in seconds, I understood the square holes cut into Neanderthal skulls that I had seen in museums and archeology magazines. I felt massive, acute pain as my skull was suddenly several sizes too small for my brain... I had to get to the hopital. In the two minutes it took my husband to get up to Labor & Delivery after parking the car, it was clear that the situation was critical. Nurses stopped him at the door: "Forget about the baby. The baby's gone. We're working to save your wife right now. There's a one in ten chance she'll survive the night."

(Spoiler alert: that baby is now a happy, bilingual, nine-year-old, soccer-playing gymnast and dancer.)

Meanwhile, I was watching myself from the ceiling. The nurses all marveled at how I had walked in on my own two feet. With a blood pressure reading like that, I should have been passed out, or at least catatonic.

There are times in life when you'll face pain so great that you almost move beyond it. This was one of those times for me. When I stopped resisting the pain, something unbelievable happened.

A voice was telling me that if I wanted to, I could just leave, and it would be very easy—a slight step off to the left: no pain, no jostling. In fact, if I did, the pain would go away. And no matter whether I chose to stay or go, the baby was going to be fine; she was a survivor.

That voice inspired such confidence that I *absolutely knew* that she was going to be okay, but I was curious to see her face, so I replied, "No, I think I'll stay." At that exact moment, of course, the scenario changed: instead of moving rapidly toward death, I started moving back into life.

That moment has stayed with me as a powerful moment of truth. "Do you trust the Universe, or do you trust what your own brain is telling you?" I threw my lot in with the Universe, and never looked back.

Birth and death were in the offing that day, but it wasn't just a baby that was born: it was a rock-solid intuitive. What died for good that day was the Warrior for Logic who had emerged from the skeptic's bootcamp nine years before; she was killed in that fateful encounter with the Divine.

This passing was not made public for years, however. I was the leader of my department, a professor, someone whom people of influence respected, so I had to keep up appearances.

The third turning point came two years later. One day at lunch, my therapist friend said, "I just had my Akashic Records channelled. You *have* to do this!"

I didn't even know what the Akashic Records were, but she insisted, and I'm forever grateful that she did. The Akashic Records are an archive of everything that your soul has ever experienced in this and all the past lifetimes, plus drafts of what's in store for you in the future. My curiosity was piqued! As a literature specialist, I had a particular weakness for archives…

"Who am I on a soul level?" was my first question in the Records. The answer: "You are a Truth Teller with capital "t"s, and when you sing your Truth Song, imprisoned angels are set free."

That blew me away. I had tears in my eyes at the beauty of this, but I was also confused. I was a French and Women's Studies professor, department chair, and scholar. What did being a Truth Teller even mean? I didn't know, but I was *hooked*.

It took me just shy of two years from that moment to implode my academic career. I left a tenured position—a guaranteed job for life—in the middle of the worst economic downturn in seventy-five years to go off and seek my fortune setting angels free with my Truth Song, and I haven't regretted it for a minute.

As a lifelong feminist, I thought teaching Women's Studies and marching in the streets for Women's Rights were the *nec plus ultra* of what I could do to promote equality and justice for womankind. Ha!

Now I empower women—imprisoned angels— around the globe through my Oracle work to know their soul truths and to live their authentic lives. As they are lifted up and their lives bettered, they create more wealth, happiness, and empowerment for all those around them. It's *viral*; I love that.

I definitely do not regret leaving the career I loved so much for so long. I'm much more powerful now and—more importantly— I'm *happy*.

How I Define Power

Power, to me, is about owning your truth, being rooted in your authenticity. Power implies depth that you can't get to if you're not owning your truth and living authentically. As a department chair I had power, but I had no idea what *real* power was at the time. Now that I'm the mouthpiece of the Divine and unearthing deep spiritual widsom that's been lost for ages… well, *that* is true power.

There are two ways to own your power, and we get to choose in every moment which way to go. The one we're most familiar with is power *over*, which is the old top-down, masculinist, or patriarchal paradigm, still evident in most corporate and institutional structures.

Conversely, there's power *to*, which is not about squashing people down, but all about lifting them up. It's not about *limiting* the options, but expanding them. This is the new model based on the Divine Feminine. It's power *among*, not power over. It's not a hierarchy, where ultimately there's a single leader or decision maker. Instead, it's the *circle*, where everyone's gifts are recognized and where every member of the circle can be a leader in her or his area of expertise. All it takes it living your authentic truth.

What Makes a Woman Powerful

Women are powerful because we have the physical bodies to be creators, whether we choose to have children or not. It's not a coincidence (there is no such thing as coincidence) that I was reborn as a powerful woman as my daughter was being born early. My intuitive powers exploded right then.

Women are powerful because we are naturally quite grounded, simply because our bodies follow the cycles of the moon and change from week to week based on what's going on around us and on the planet.

Women are powerful because we allow ourselves to be more connected to our intuitions. Men can be just as intuitive as women, but most men are taught that you don't touch intuition with a ten-foot pole. (Perhaps it's a karmic fear of being burned at the stake.)

Women are powerful because we are the reflection of the Goddess. The Goddess made flesh.

So here's the capital-T Truth: Not only are we enough—*we are amazing.*

Tools for Connecting to Your Feminine Power

These tips are a reflection of that which, in my worldview, makes women powerful:

Firstly, *connect to—and use—your intuition.* Tap into your Oracle Powers. If you want to fast-track this, I suggest consulting your Akashic Records: the on-demand source of your intuitive information. Go hire an Oracle to help you get to your Truth. When you hear it, your Truth will heal issues that have been confusing you or holding you back for decades.

Secondly, *connect to Mother Earth.* For the many decades now, we've been prevented from doing this with our asphalted roads and rubber- or plastic-soled shoes. The Earth is a gift, and you'll find that if you get outside on the ground without shoes for a few minutes several times per day, your life will be better.

You'll be less frazzled, more centered, and better able to handle the demands of the day. I'm also a big proponent of tree-hugging, especially if being barefoot isn't feasible.

Thirdly, *connect with other women.* The symbol of the Feminine Divine is the circle. So, create circles of women for support in your life. Really reach out. Sisterhood is powerful.

Finally, *connect to your own sexiness.* Really *own* it! Even if you don't believe that you're sexy, you are—your wisdom and depth bring incredible sensuality. Sensuality is a highly charged woman's power at any age.

It's also important not to put everyone first and end up losing yourself. I have to raise my hand as someone who did fall prey to that, especially once I stepped into owning and running a business that I was passionate about. Sometimes I was my own lowest priority. On the top rung of my priorities were my business and my family— especially my daughter—followed by making the house run properly and *then* self care. I really learned the hard way that *that just can't happen,* so you need to stop and look around.

There is such power in stopping, in stillness. This is why meditation as a practice is great. I got away from it when my business got super, super busy. I went from meditating daily, to every so often, to not very often at all. At that point, things started piling up; I would feel overwhelmed, make mistakes, and not feel good about myself because of them.

All it takes is making a promise to hold onto your special, sacred, personal time. For me it has to do with connecting with nature—taking a walk, standing outside and pulling in the power from the Earth through the bare soles of my feet, hugging a tree, and just feeling that energy pour into me. In those moments, I know that I am not alone, that in my connection to the whole planet, the Universe, and everything else that there might be on a subatomic level, I have access to limitless resources.

In that stillness, I can look around, and say, "Oh, right. It's not so important that I finish X activity today. What's really important is that I look deep into my heart and see exactly the right thing to do and exactly the best way for me to unfold my day." And that's true of anything.

You can't be your most brilliant you if you are worn out, run ragged, and too tired to own your power. So, really, what it takes is stopping and pulling in power from the Universe. Power, wisdom, knowledge, peace. And then, from that place of stillness and power, stepping forward into the world. When you're in that place, you can be more generous. You're not going to judge yourself or others so much. You're not going to feel overwhelmed. You're not going to try to control everything. (I'm a recovering control freak—I know what I'm talking about.)

So *stop*. Especially when things get really, really busy. That's when you absolutely, *imperatively* must stop. You *must* slow down. Rushing is antithetical to spiritual existence, and I've fallen into rushing in my life several times. Fortunately, I think I learned my lesson this year.

You can actually get more done with stillness—it's true. Here's a story from my department chair days: Every day I would go in to the office and then I'd take an hour off to go meditate with a circle of women. Afterwards, I would be super-productive. But on some really busy days, I might skip the meditation because I had "too much to do." Alas, I was never as effective if I hadn't had my morning meditation!

Stillness is super important. It's not going to slow you down. It's actually going to *ground* you so that you can be more effective, more powerful, more present. And, of course, presence is the space of enlightenment. Enlightenment isn't the destination at the far end of the road. You can be in that place of enlightenment whenever you like by choosing to slow down and be fully present to where you are, what you're doing, who you're with. Remember: it's always a choice.

Our New Role as Women and Our Challenges

I think our new role as women is to be leaders of the world. The Dalai Lama said it best: "The world will be saved by the Western woman." We have been the leaders of the world in the background, and now we are reclaiming our rightful place in the foreground. For several thousand years, women have been leading from behind men as best we could, and now it's time for us to stop the madness and start owning our power, to start speaking our Truth.

Under millenia of patriarchy, we've seen "progess," and we've also seen massive oppression and destruction. Through industrialization and competition, we have driven our planet to the brink of environmental catastrophe. It's time—past time—to start operating from a sense of cooperation and shared responsibilities and resources if we're going to survive.

Let's get clear and understand what's really at stake. Following our current path guarantees our destruction—perhaps even in this century. If the mothers ran the planet and treated it and everyone on it as family, wars and environmental degradation would cease.

Please don't fool yourself into thinking you're not a leader because you're "just a mom." (I want to banish that phrase from the English language.) You *are* a leader. And please don't diminish the power of being a mother. When I saw the Dalai Lama speak revently, he extolled his mother at great length. Essentially, he claims to be who he is today because of her—her patience, her goodwill, her generosity. It was so inspiring. So you're never "just" a mom or "just" *anything*. You are absolutely *who you are*—powerful, seductive, gorgeous… the Goddess made flesh.

Our biggest challenge as women is seeing ourselves as we truly are—magnificent beings who are capable of creating new life, and businesses, and anything else that pops into our brilliant minds. (Incidentally, the Akashic Records can correct this misconception for you if it is holding you back.) We are *all* the Goddess made flesh. For better or for worse, we have been told all our lives that we're insufficient: that we're too fat or too skinny; that we're too weak, stupid or even crazy.

Women who have powerful ideas are called crazy all the time. Those who insist on owning their power are called crazy, or bossy at best. It would be ridiculous to call a man "bossy": that's just how he's "supposed to" be. But women can be diminished—cut down to size—by being called bossy because, of course, women aren't "supposed to" be powerful.

It's time to change that. It's time to reclaim our power as women.

Historically, women were venerated as the Goddess made flesh—which we still are, of course, but we have been taught that we are so much less.

This shift occurred thanks to patriarchal power plays in Athens and Rome. Ancient Greece and Athens in particular are held up as the birthplace of western civilization, yet it was the Greeks who worked to break up Earth Goddess Gaia's power by fragmenting her. (Women are still fragmented in the media—look at print ads; we are often represented as headless body parts: see Jean Kilbourne's "Killing Us Softly" documentaries for an assessment that will floor you.)

Instead of the all-powerful Source of Creation, The Goddess was broken down into a series of smaller Goddesses relegated to lesser positions as lovers and wives of Greek Gods, who held dominion over them. Incidentally, this is when humanity became separated from the Divine—when the Divine was no longer under our feet, in the people and animals who shared our lives, and in the food we ate, but "out there" in the heavens, it became inaccessible, and we started to feel cut off or separate from our Divine Power.

Gaia's beauty and sensuality was split off as Aphrodite; her wisdom and strength was split off as Athena; the nurturing Earth mother aspect became Demeter; her fierce wildness and animality was split off into Artemis…. That was the beginning of the end of the Goddess worship on this planet.

Once the Greeks had weakened her, it was easy for the Judeo-Christians, and especially the Church of Rome, to finish the job. The apple and the snake—tools of the priestesses of Aphrodite/ Venus—became symbols of the Fall. Priestesses whose holy duty was to help people to connect with the Divine were recast as prostitutes—criminals.

The one nod to divinity in feminine form had to become a sexless virgin. The other faces of the Goddess, especially her

94

sensual side, had to be reviled. So, the Goddess was repainted as Eve: instead of being the most powerful creatrix, the most beautiful goddess in existence, she was cast as a stupid, evil woman, and her "sin" (using the tools of the Goddess) remained a punishment for women for all time. In this way, stupid and evil got packed inside the very *idea* of woman.

It's just a measure of the power of women that it took such a concerted effort on the part of patriarchy, for thousands of years, to put us in a box! Now we're coming back out and saying to the patriacrchal system: "Enough. We've let you spin these false stories long enough, and it's time to take our Power back. Not just because it's right to set things straight, but because you are about to ruin this beautiful, sacred planet. Enough fighting. Enough destruction. Go connect to your feminine side—tap into your intuition and your connection with others—and the world will be a better place."

In closing, I want to remind everyone reading this (men as well as women) that You. Are. Divine.

If you don't believe it, I want you to start looking for the presence—and the *presents*—of the Universe in your life every day. Look for evidence that you are Divine. That evidence can be synchonicities (you may know them as "coincidences"), messages from animals, the beauty of nature around you, or the voices of children. You are Divine! My role on the planet this time around is to be a leader of women, and to remind you that you are Divine, so *enjoy* your beauty. I see it, and I *love* it.

CHAPTER 7

Celia Ward-Wallace

Celia Ward-Wallace is a Certified Life & Business Coach, Inspirational Speaker and the Author of "A Woman's Guide to Having it All, Life Lessons to Live By." Celia thought she had the perfect life – until she lost it all. Through her journey back from rock bottom, she realized that a great life is not measured by what you have but by who you are. Celia Ward-Wallace is on a mission to mobilize over 1,000,000 women with the tools to stand in their power, live a life of contribution and manifest their greatness. Celia empowers the modern every day woman as the founder of the international women's community Empowering Women Every Day and the creator of the signature live event Women's Night Out. Celia also partners with major brands who LOVE women such as Starbucks, Johnson & Johnson and the Honest Company providing transformational products, events and training. Celia also certifies women as Life & Business Coaches as the Vice President of the Certified Coaches Federation and leads female entrepreneurs to create online businesses they love through The Super Fly Soulful Business Mastery Program. Learn more at http://www.CeliaWardWallace.com.

My Story and My Journey to Power

Remembering My Privilege. When I reflect on my journey to power, I am very aware that I am a woman of privilege living in the United States situated within the global world of women. I was raised in the inner city of L.A., surrounded by people of diverse cultures, religions and languages because of the commitment my parents had to inner-city life and the work they did as civil-rights organizers. As a result, I grew up in a beautiful environment focused on tolerance and open-mindedness, an environment that encouraged people to be leaders and stand in their power, step into everything that they were given, and speak their minds about whatever they believed. The culture was built on the principle that it was important to stand up for equality and justice as well as challenge those who were abusing their power as bosses, politicians, police, etc. The goal was to create positive change through individual and community empowerment.

It wasn't difficult for me to connect with my power as a woman because I come from a family of extremely powerful women going back multiple generations—women who stepped into their greatness, who really stood in their power and used their voices to impact positive change in the world, whether that was within their homes, within their communities, or within their political environment. My great-great-grandmother Melinda led her family across the country in a wagon train and later wrote the women's rights column for her local newspaper. Later, her daughters traveled around the world and marched for women's right to vote, which was finally won in 1920. My great-great-grandmother Elizabeth worked to send all four of her daughters to college. My great-great-grandmother Sarah fled the pogroms in

Russia and became a garment worker in New York and a member of the International Ladies Garment Workers Union. My mother and grandmothers came out of the feminist movement of the 1960s and 70s and dedicated a large portion of their lives to fighting on behalf of women's liberation: the right of women to step into their power, feel confident with their ambition and their desire to be equal, and have their voices to be heard. My mom worked every day and dedicated her life to social justice and the empowerment of women and all people. So from early on, there were powerful women who were strong role models in my life—women who owned their power, became leaders, and loved that about themselves.

Equality and tolerance have been themes throughout my life. In high school and college I applied my power and privilege to uplifting others, especially people of color and women. I studied inner-group conflict and prejudice; I created unity activism support groups in school around race, class, and gender issues. As captain of my high school women's basketball team, I learned how to work with women of diverse backgrounds as well as came to understand the power that women's sports create. I graduated from UCLA with joint degrees in sociology and world arts and cultures.

Facing My Challenges

I grew up in a household with an abundance of love, and while we were not poor, we did not have an abundance of money either. After attending UCLA, I began to have a lot of money anxiety and adopted a scarcity mentality. I graduated without debt but immediately had to support myself. I tried quickly to find the safest job I could get that would provide a regular paycheck, benefits and pension—everything I thought I needed to feel whole and safe. I had worked throughout college with intramural sports, so right out of college I began working as a Community Center Director with a particular responsibility to build the girls' and women's sports programs and enforce Title IX gender equity laws. Being a Community Center Director was part of a wonderful profession—community building through sports and recreation. But after a few years I became unhappy and unfulfilled. I knew that I was not living my purpose, but I still stayed there for over ten years out of fear and uncertainty. I went to law school at night for four years, seeking intellectual stimulation and possibly a better avenue for social change. I earned my Doctor of Jurisprudence, but also learned the immense restrictions of the law. It was not the vehicle for change I'd hoped it would be.

During that time, I met my husband, who was an entrepreneur. We fell in love and, both of us still searching, we began to invest in real estate part time. We went from buying one small piece of property to, over a course of years, building a multimillion-dollar real estate business at the height of the boom of the real estate market.

You would think that between having the "safe" public-sector job and having all this power, money, and achievement at my disposal, I would have felt happy. But in reality I was the most stressed-out version of myself ever and wasn't in tune with the rhythm of the universe, the rhythm of my soul, and the calling and purpose for my life.

I often say that the universe sends us messages and that first they begin as whispers. If you don't hear them, they get a little bit louder, and if you still don't hear them they get a little bit louder, and eventually the messages need to yell at you in the form of something drastic happening in your life to wake you up. For me, the wake-up call was a combination of crises in my life, both personally and financially. Essentially the combination of the real estate market crash, my husband having a career-ending injury, and facing bankruptcy, foreclosure, and complete financial loss was the wake-up call. We were in darkness, living with financial strain, personal stress, anxiety, and depression for over five years. We played the blame game and the "would-have, should-have, and could-have" regret game. Eventually, through tremendous self-growth and faith, we both began to heal and learn from our lessons. During this time, my husband and I grew very close and I gave birth to two joy-filled girls. I began to see the light.

Finding My Purpose

I was a mother, a wife, a daughter, and a granddaughter. I was a basketball coach to adult women and little girls. I was living many roles and had many responsibilities. I was very self-reliant and didn't ask others for help or let my support system know about the hardships I was facing. I didn't let my friends know. I was desperate for a solution, a way to make sense of my pain and to not feel alone. This led me on a journey of introspection, healing and reinvention, much of which came through regular counseling and daily spiritual practice. Like my parents and grandparents before me, I have been a life-long searcher. I have always had a love of learning, so I started to study world religions and spirituality. I started to do all of the amazing daily practices that I feel really ground us in our energy and personal power, such as meditation, prayer, intention setting and affirmations, yoga, exercise, connecting with nature, and connecting with people. By prioritizing these practices, I was able to transform the negative programming I had in my head about limiting beliefs and fears, worries and doubts. Over time, this journey helped me manifest the power that I had within myself. It was a beautiful, feminine power of self-acceptance, of tolerance of others, and of intuition and connection with nature, myself, and my world. Through embracing the journey and practicing self-care and spirituality, I found my purpose. I realized that all of my life experiences had happened for a reason. They were the experiences I needed to have in order to share my story with others who were going through the same thing. The lifelong skills of speaking, writing, leadership, community building, and cultural integration all led me to where I am today, working in the field of coaching, writing, and speaking.

Chasing My Dream

I realize now that every bit of power and strength I have within me has been instilled through my genetics, from my ancestors, and by my upbringing. All came together to form a perfect gift of aligning me with the field of coaching and becoming a leader in the world around life, business, and spirituality. I created a business around my unique talents, experiences, and passions to help other women be able to do the same thing.

My work as a life and business coach primarily centers on helping women realize their power, privilege, and potential. Through sharing the lessons I have learned, I teach them how to develop practices to change their daily life. I show them how to make very small—but over time, massive—life transformations for themselves, their families, and their communities. I also wrote a book, *A Woman's Guide to Having It All, Life Lessons To Live By*, my love letter to all of the women of the world, which says: "On the outside it may look like I have it all, but it took me a long time to get here. Here's all the crap that I was dealing with and had to get through, all the lessons that I've learned that were invaluable to me. And I continue to love my true power as a woman."

How I Define Power

I define personal power as an alignment within—when you are really on track, on purpose. Power comes from being completely authentic and true to yourself and loving yourself completely. This should be a woman's guiding force in life. When this happens, you will always pay attention to what your feelings and instincts are telling you. Then you can step forth with conscious intention and manifest results.

I've always been familiar with this personal power, and in some ways I've had to wrestle with my power. My mother told me that as a young girl she was afraid she would be too powerful— an experience I also had. Being powerful while compelling is also something that society often discourages and vilifies within women, which can be very challenging.

Many cultures and spiritual traditions have concepts like the Taoist yin-yang, which helps us to understand the whole dialectic of masculine and feminine power that we all have within. Men carry both masculine and feminine powers, as do women. A powerful person accesses both the masculine and the feminine powers to create an abundant life full of creativity, intention, and joy. In fact, people occupy a wide variety of balances between masculine and feminine.

Unfortunately, our social systems foster an overarching social structure of patriarchy and sexism. This structure takes the masculine and feminine aspects of all humans and splits them so that MAN is masculine and WOMAN is feminine. Systematic sexism oppresses—so seeking to discover our balance entails fighting against both internalized oppression and external institutions.

As women, we have a lot of aptitudes, especially the modern woman who has taken on a lot of responsibilities typically seen as masculine. She may be in the workplace more, or making more money, or have a lot more demands on her life. Women have the skills to plan, take action, be successful, be in charge, be in control, go through lists, make things happen, be the boss, etc. It's fantastic, but it pulls at you from both the masculine and the feminine side.

If we lean too heavily on our sacred masculine power and operate on overdrive, we suffer, becoming burned out and resentful. We end up doing so much that we lose sight of the whole other beautiful side of ourselves, which is really where I feel the divine feminine power comes from. This is the softer, more intuitive, side of who we are—the part which requires becoming quieter, going within to listen to our inner voice, and connecting with nature. Instead of taking action, we need to allow ourselves to receive what our actions have created. Women, we have done all this work. Now we need to sit still and see what's going to come back to us instead of just continuing to go into overdrive.

What Makes a Woman Powerful

What makes a woman so powerful is her heart. Women are powerful because within every fiber of our being we see the world through the eyes of love. A woman's number one instinct is to love, nurture, and help others prosper. We give of ourselves selflessly.

Although generosity and compassion are some of women's greatest powers, they can also work to the detriment of women. Sometimes we give too much of ourselves without leaving enough in reserve for our own self-care. Women must understand how to use this power for their own good as well. To really be able to do what I call, "stepping into your power" or "stepping into your greatness," and discover your calling requires ultimately loving yourself and accepting yourself exactly as you are. You must quiet the inner critic and the negative self-talk and not go to a place of blame, shame, and judgment of yourself. Instead, give to yourself all of that compassion and generosity and patience that you give to every other person.

When women can fill up their own spirits with love, we demonstrate true feminine power. Then, when we give to others, we can give abundantly and compassionately and also understand the boundaries and limitations of what we want in our lives. We are able to communicate clearly with others about our feelings of potentially being overextended, or taken advantage of. It's really a retraining of the mind to give yourself what you give to others.

We need to realize that power comes from within us, and that the only things we have the power to control are the thoughts in our head—which result in associated feelings, actions and results. When we focus on creating alignment between our conscious and unconscious minds with positive thoughts, we can reprogram our minds to create alignment in our life. Then, we will have positive and empowered feelings. This power is within us, and we create the life that we want to have as a result of it.

Tools to Connecting to Your Feminine Power

Unearthing My Own Feminine Power. I was able to connect with my feminine power when I tapped back into the traditions of the female ancestors many, many generations before me—communal living, sisterhood support, oneness with the universe and all there is, conscious parenting, fearless loving, and connection with nature.

I am a mother of two young daughters. The joy of being a mom and the responsibility of being a conscious parent teaches me that everything I do with them, every conversation I have, and every action that I take shapes them. This empowers me to be the best that I can be as a woman and to model for them that I love my feminine power. I want nothing more than for them to grow to be powerful, conscious, and enlightened young women who stand as leaders in their workplaces, homes, and communities. I also learn so much from them; as much as I teach them, they also teach me every moment as well. They remind me that life is about joy, unlimited possibility, and compassion. What a blessing and gift to be a mother!

My best practices for connecting with your feminine power are to make the time to slow down, take nature walks or sit in your backyard looking at butterflies and just listening to the birds, do yoga or mediation, write in a journal writing, watch TV, or hang out with your girlfriends laughing or dancing all night. These are things that bring us back to balance and allow our feminine power to fill us up and bring us back to the true essence of who we are.

Creating My Feminism

While we strive to balance the masculine and feminine aspects within ourselves, to love ourselves, and to embrace our personal feminine power, we inevitably hit the wall of sexism every day. It holds women down, it abuses them, and it cheats them. We can see the culture silently placing chains around our daughters. My mother saw this as my sisters and I went through adolescence. She nurtured our feminine power as individuals, but she also taught us that we would need to join together with other women, and supportive men, to create feminism—a collective action against an oppressive system that subjugates women around the world. Along my journey, as I harnessed my personal feminine power, I understood that my purpose was to organize women collectively and to create feminisms—not one, but many—based on the many different conditions women face around the world. Feminisms are the variety of collective actions that can dismantle institutionalized sexism.

I began the "Empowering Women Every Day Community," an international community oriented towards empowering and mobilizing over one million women to stand in their feminine power and to live a life of contribution—to manifest the greatness that is within every one of us. Together we can strengthen each other and create our feminism.

Remembering Not to Forget Yourself

I'm an entrepreneur, and I have two little girls. I'm a wife, daughter, granddaughter, and landlord, and I'm very active in my community—leading neighborhood cleanups, volunteering at my children's school, and coaching my children's soccer and basketball teams. So there are many roles and unlimited demands in my life. I am able to overcome the tendency to put myself last by prioritizing self-care as a role in itself. Each week when I schedule my time, I make self-care a non-negotiable priority. As a life coach I have learned that as much as I adore my family and my work, I also adore myself. I am no good to my family, my work, or my community if I am not in a good place mentally, physically and spiritually. Therefore, when I look at each week, I break down somewhere between six to ten different roles that I want to play that week, and I include "self-care" as a role. Then I make sure that for each one of those roles or identities I choose two or three things that week that I need to do to create harmony in my life. I write them down, actually scheduling them as non-negotiable appointments. When I practice self-care and self-love, I am powerful.

Now, it's not a perfect system. There are weeks when work is on overdrive or I'm exhausted from the kids. But because I work to be conscious and awake to my life, I can tell when I'm starting to get tense, tired, or overextended, turning into that cranky wife who is nagging my husband or being short-tempered with my kids, having no patience, or being reactive to them. Then I am not being the true essence of who I am or operating from my higher self, and I am very aware that something's got to change. This may mean that I have to slow down, look at my week and maybe block off a full day just for me to focus on myself, stay in my pajamas while the kids are at school, or have a date with my couch and the TV. These are simple things, but it's the simple things that make a difference.

Our New Role as Women and Our Challenges

Our new role as women is to step into our feminine power, to step into our greatness, and to lead the world—to not be in fear any longer of playing big or going after the opportunities that set our heart on fire and excite us. It is really about just waking up and realizing that this is our life to live and lead by example in a big way, showing everybody around us that we are happy and that fulfillment and love are a priority. These are the things that life is all about! As we leverage our power, privilege and leadership with this message, we will offer something new and transformative to humanity. This model of feminism is really where we need to go to help change the world.

One challenge in our society is that everything's speeding up. We have to work harder and make more money. Our whole lives are turned upside down because we're taking on more and more demands and more and more roles. It's so important that we approach our lives in a conscious way. When I say "conscious," I mean being awake, paying attention to each moment, and making decisions mindfully, openly and intentionally instead of just letting life happen to you.

It is difficult to balance and self-care while also asking for help by releasing some power and responsibilities to those around us. This means that as you are faced with the challenges, you need to be aware of what is happening, thinking through and making decisions that feel best for you in the moment on an authentic, intuitional level. Basically, you do the best you can. Then, whatever happens as a result, you pay attention to that as well and make adjustments along the way. The more you're able to do this and pay attention to what's happening within you and around you, the more quickly you can get to a place where you are in flow and using your feminine power and your natural gifts and abilities—a place where your life is really everything you imagined it to be. This does not mean that your life is without challenges, but it means you are feeling that you've got it figured out and you can make it work. Then you truly feel fulfilled and happy.

Shifting gender and household dynamics can also be challenging. Women have a wide variety of experiences and gender identities. Many women are now in same-sex relationships. We all face the same system of patriarchy and we are all part of a common sisterhood. For those of us who are in heterosexual relationships, there definitely are some challenges about the amount of power and accomplishment that women are able to attain now and how the role of the woman in the home has pretty much done a complete 180-degree turn. Household dynamics are definitely shifting and becoming more complicated to navigate. This has left a lot of men wondering where they fit into this new picture and what their roles and responsibilities are. Can women release some of their responsibilities?

Lastly, we all need to know that we are worthy and good enough. We are already blessed to be created and be here in this lifetime. Now is the time for us to shed any limiting beliefs that were put on us by our parents, by our religion, by our teachers, or by a patriarchal society about what being a woman means, what a woman can achieve, or what a woman can have in her life. It's really the time to break free of all of the shackles and step into our greatness; we don't need to be anything other than exactly who we are right now.

You are worthy; you are perfect exactly as you are. Look at yourself in the mirror and say, "I love you, I forgive you and I accept you." Be happy and live a life of gratitude for all of the simple and wonderful things that are happening in your life. Realize that each and every moment you have is a blessing and something to be grateful for. Don't think that you need to have anything else or do anything else to get to a place where you can finally like yourself. Instead, know that you are 100 percent complete. You've got it, girl! You've got everything that you need; all you need now is to celebrate—love yourself!

"Having it all" means realizing that we already have everything we need within us. We can become whole and complete when we feel love, our feminine power, our greatness, gratitude, beauty, and blessings—everything is already there within ourselves. Nobody can ever take that from us!

CHAPTER 8

Jessica Riverson

A successful entrepreneur since 1999, Permission to Charge™ Mentor, Jessica Riverson transforms the businesses of heart-centered consultants, coaches and service providers whose passion for helping others stands in their way of charging and receiving their worth. Jessica is a respected speaker, business coach, and the CEO and Founder of Permission to Charge™, an International coaching and training company serving highly compassionate and highly ambitious women who want to ask for what they're worth and get it. She is a Certified Money Breakthrough Coach© and the author of "Permission to Charge." Jessica's group and private programs are designed to teach critical money mindset and business skills to empower women to go from feeling like "I can't charge that" to "Oh yes I can!" Through her proprietary and proven 3-step process, her clients create multiple six figure businesses by learning to charge their worth, package their expertise and re-define sales as service, so they can profit and serve for a lifetime. To get free tools and resources to double your income from Jessica, please visit www.jessicariverson.com.

My Story and My Journey to Power

My life evolved from being a single mom to being a business coaching and training company franchise owner. I began my life as a single mom at eighteen years old and was a single mom for the next twelve to thirteen years of my child's life.

I come from four generations of single moms—my great grandmother lost her husband during World War II when her children were very young, and she had to enter a refugee camp and journey to the United States; my grandmother had my mom when she was nineteen; my mom had me when she was seventeen; and then I had my son when I was eighteen. This is not a legacy that I want to perpetuate, but I've learned a lot about strength from this lineage.

But first, I want to take you back to the beginning—my beginning. When I was young, I used to spend a lot of time thinking. I can remember sitting at my desk in my room all alone, thinking and journaling about what life was really all about. I figured I must be pretty weird to spend so much time pondering life, and I wasn't sure if my friends were doing the same. I was also very inquisitive about religion and spirituality. I was always trying to figure out the meaning of life. At fifteen, I began reading books by authors like Wayne Dyer and Deepak Chopra. My spiritual foundation was being developed.

Everyone needs a wake-up call in life to jolt her into her intended journey. My wake-up call in life came when I became a mother. For someone else it might be a completely different wakeup call, but for me this was it. I very quickly realized I had to figure life out. It felt very urgent, and I began reading even more books and trying to learn about everything I could do to better myself. I always really believed in personal growth and having a mentor. So, when I was nineteen, I hired my first coach. The majority of my coaches were women. I think this was the key to my success—having the support system and really investing in myself that way.

Through this process of growing up so fast and moving through life's challenges, I was essentially learning what I was made of. This is the point at which I began connecting with my feminine power. Once you become a parent, you don't have much freedom to just explore; you've got to learn about yourself while you're raising someone else. And that's very difficult. I experienced some really hard parenting years. Not only was I single mom, but there also wasn't any manual for this particular kid, who had some serious behavioral and developmental issues.

I thank God every day that my husband came into my son's life when he did. The challenges that I faced—learning to be financially responsible and having to figure out a very different kid and how to raise him—made me stronger and more convinced that I could overcome adversity. I also desperately struggled with how to break through my own self-esteem issues. I think that's what prompted me to start my journey of seeking even as a teenager. I knew there was a better way to take care of myself and treat myself. I saw that my parents—my mom and my stepdad— had a great relationship, so I tried to figure out why I was choosing bad relationships and also not loving myself, as I'd practiced self-loathing and self-hatred for years.

It was a very difficult mindset to break, the mindset of unworthiness. I treated myself and allowed myself to be treated by others in extremely destructive ways. I struggled with an eating disorder and struggled with attracting men who lied, cheated, and were emotionally abusive to me. It took ten to fifteen years to attempt to break through, and in the end I had to learn to love myself.

Later in my journey, I began to learn even more about myself. I could not believe how a course on money could help my self-worth, but it dealt with the connection between self-worth and net worth. In this money program, one that I now teach, the paradigm presented was "How you do money is how you do everything." I started to see how that was true, and I evaluated my behavior patterns—how I did relationships, how I did money, how I did health, how I did my business, and how I did parenting. In all of it, I saw an extreme lack of boundaries. This recognition and the work I did that followed allowed me to break through, and I'm still breaking through. This is a journey we're all on.

How I Define Power

When I think of the word "power," I think of strength—having a solid foundation or having a solid ground to stand on. The word "power" is connected to the word empowered—so if you're empowered, you feel that you're confident—that you have the capacity to move forward in your life—and you feel that you can go for what you want. It also means you're not a victim; you're not making excuses. You take total responsibility for yourself. There were countless times when I felt very powerless—lying in a puddle of tears on the floor. But I always dusted myself off and came back to that center focusing on spirit and God. I'd sometimes ask the question, "What does my higher self want?" This would connect me to a higher consciousness instead of just thinking and feeling.

Often we just go off of our emotions, but that's not your true self talking, and it's not God talking to you either. That's your Ego! I always feel powerful when I can first let go and realize that pain and suffering isn't getting me anywhere anyway. Then, I press my reset button. Perhaps it's praying or meditating or having a quiet moment where you can connect that resets you. For me, God is whom I connect with.

What Makes a Woman Powerful

There are two things that make a woman powerful: confidence and forgiveness. A woman who stands in her truth, right or wrong, good or bad, is confident because she owns it. This confidence also allows the woman to believe in herself, not make excuses, and take responsibility for her actions.

A woman's ability to forgive also makes her powerful. I have felt like there were all these people who had done me wrong and that I needed to forgive them. I discovered we have to forgive ourselves and that through doing that we can be empowered. Interestingly enough, I also discovered that forgiveness is not necessarily a one-shot deal. I'd thought I could just forgive myself once and then voilà, I'd be done. But it turns out that I forgive myself every day and hold kindness for myself. It's a journey. Continue to be compassionate with yourself, forgive yourself for past mistakes, and forgive the mistakes of others against you.

Maybe someone told you, "You're stupid" or "You're not good enough." You accepted it, and now you've been operating as if that was the truth. This limits us in life. The key is to forgive ourselves for believing in those untruths and making those unconscious agreements. It's not even really about forgiving the person who gave us that message; it's about telling yourself that it's not your truth and it doesn't serve you anymore. Forgive yourself. Definitely part of power is confidence, but if you have the ability to forgive, I believe you are even more powerful.

Tools for Connecting to Your Feminine Power

So, how does a powerful woman make that connection to her power? Women must understand that power doesn't come from giving themselves to others until there's nothing left of themselves to give. I'm reminded of a quote from Abraham Hicks that says, "You cannot get sick enough to help sick people get better. You cannot get poor enough to help poor people thrive. It's only in your thriving that you have anything to offer anyone. If you're wanting to be of an advantage to others, be as tapped in, tuned in, turned in as you can possibly be." In other words, you can't be a martyr. You can't devalue yourself so much for the sake of others because there won't be anything left.

I used to do that in my romantic relationships. It was all about the other person, and I was trampled on emotionally. In those situations I had no power. Back then, being the woman meant I came second and that I wasn't as important. I no longer believe this or live that way. *A woman connects with her power when she values herself.* Women, because we are natural givers, sometimes lose ourselves in our work or our marriage or our kids, and we forget about ourselves. You have to make time for yourself and keep it like an important date.

For women to be tapped into their own power, they must seek what pleasures them. They must choose what makes them happy and have the time to pursue it. If you're in a relationship and that's something that's important to you and you want it to grow, then have that date with that person. If you're working at home or you're just a really busy mom or a busy career woman, set aside a day in the week for some alone time. Don't let life get in the way; make those important dates with yourself, with your spouse, and with your kids. There are just so many things and so many people vying for your time. We have to keep what really matters at the center.

Through my time learning from a personal development coach and attending trainings, I learned that just because you purposefully take time for yourself doesn't mean that you're a bad person or selfish, or that you don't care about other people. I'm passionate about what I do, so I've done a pretty good job of making sure that I do follow my dreams and I do put the things that matter to me first. It is very hard to be the sole person responsible financially for raising a child, but I do pursue the things in my life that I enjoy.

Our New Role as Women and Our Challenges

Women's role in society is constantly changing. This change enables women to create better connections with other women. The Dalai Lama once said, "The world will be saved by the Western Woman." I tend to agree with him. Women are feeling more and more empowered to look outside our own homes and our own community, and now with technology we can even connect with women in a remote village somewhere. We can find out what our interests are and we can do things that support them. This connection to others helps us to grow into this new role and connect with each other.

As women, we have a lot of power, influence, ability, and responsibility. Great responsibility, however, can also sometimes bring great challenges. A very high percentage of women are now the breadwinners for their family, for example. They are wearing the pants, and yet they're still wearing the apron, the nursing bra, the lingerie, and the high heels. Just think of all the different outfits that we put on!

I believe that even though we have a lot on our collective plate, we also need time to reflect on who we are. I think a lot of women out there are simply trying to answer the questions: Who am I? What do I want? What do I want to create? What is my legacy? What kind of relationship do I choose? How can I have it all?

This last question is a huge challenge because it's difficult to have it all. Instead of trying to "have it all," women, you must see the value of your self-worth.

For me, understanding the value of my self-worth came about through, as I mentioned earlier, understanding my relationship with money—a challenge for many women.

Throughout my twenties I began to have financial success and began learning about investing and the right steps to take with money. Unfortunately, instead of following all the good advice I was getting, I ended up creating debt and wasting money. After years of frustration, I finally looked around and asked myself, "Where is all the money?" I saw a windfall of thousands of dollars had slipped through my fingers, and I was riddled with guilt. It dawned on me that in all the personal growth courses I had taken, spending thousands and thousands of dollars, I had never really learned to master my relationship with money. I had read all the books and met with countless financial planners. I knew what I was supposed to do with money, but knowing what to do is simply worthless without the emotional integrity to follow through. I was getting close to turning thirty, and I felt like I would never be any different; I would never have a balance on my savings account or get out of debt. This was just my life, I thought.

Fortunately, all that changed when I learned the Money Breakthrough Method © curriculum, which I am now blessed to teach to others. I now have a larger savings than I've ever had in my life. I track my income and have now paid off all my credit card debt. I began to use the tools and saw changes not only in my relationship with money, but in my relationships with everyone around me.

Understanding the value of money helped me to understand my own value—connecting self-worth to net worth. Believe in yourself enough to take action in your life. Success is a lot easier to achieve when you take the first step. Your self-worth is connected to your success in all areas of your life.

CHAPTER 9

Dr. Phyllis Hubbard

Dr. Phyl is the ultimate Body Whisperer and the Founder of Radiant Health Strategies, LLC. She is a Motivational Speaker, Board Certified Naturopathic Doctor, an Ayurvedic Practitioner, Life and Health Coach, Qigong Instructor, Reiki Master and Licensed Massage Therapist (#MA64036). Her wide range of professional education also includes Holistic Health Education, Therapeutic Nutrition, Clinical Aromatherapy and Herbology. Her straightforward and humorous presentations blend ancient holistic wisdom with cutting edge research in a way that is fun and easy to understand, and she continually researches indigenous holistic practices to integrate into her healing techniques and workshops.

Having used holistic healing strategies to eliminate the medication for and completely heal herself of a supposedly incurable illness (COPD - Chronic Obstructive Pulmonary Disease), Dr. Phyl now develops and provides health prevention and intervention programs that help correct and restore imbalances in the mind and body through a synergistic blend of holistic healing modalities.

Learn more at www.radianthealthstrategies.com.

My Story and My Journey to Power

Although I realize now that it started in childhood, I became aware of my journey to power in my late twenties. Something inside me was trying to awaken. I didn't understand what it was at the time, but I knew that there was something very wrong with my world. There had always been.

My parents were teenagers when I was born, and they divorced when I was eight years old. My mother was a "nervous Nelly"—unstable and likely to fly into a panic at any time about anything. When I was with her, I worried constantly, too: "How will we pay the bills? What are we going to do?" I was the epitome of the adult child.

When I visited my father in the summertime, I felt more at ease, like I could just be a kid. Though he was a source of stability, he was also a control freak, so my view of the world when I was with him was distorted. He wasn't the type of person you could talk to about emotional issues—and of course I couldn't talk to my emotionally unstable mother about such things, either—so I learned at a very early age that if anything bad happened, I had to keep it to myself.

I looked after my mother whenever she was sick, and, truly playing out the role of the "adult child," I also looked after children who got picked on in the neighborhood. Once such child (I'll call her BB) had the same babysitter as me. BB was five years old at the time, and I was seven. I was concerned for her yet irritated by her because in a way she reminded me of my mother. She was easily manipulated; kids took advantage of her gullibility. I was especially concerned about a White boy I'd seen around—a rarity in our mostly Black and Brown neighborhood—who looked like a thirteen-year-old Billy Idol, with his platinum blond hair, pale skin and a sneaky smirk. I was too young to understand what the word "predator" meant, but I knew he was always circling our neighborhood like a shark looking for prey.

One day when I got back from school, I couldn't find BB. She wasn't out in the backyard as usual, and I intuitively knew something was wrong. I looked all through the babysitter's house and ran up and down the street shouting her name. Finally, a young boy heard me calling her name. He was coming up from the ditch where we sometimes played.

"Have you seen BB?" I asked, totally out of breath.

"She's down in the ditch with that White boy," he told me.

I don't remember running to the ditch. I only remember arriving there and coming to an abrupt stop when I saw them together. I really didn't know what I was looking at—I didn't know the word "rape"—but I knew that he was hurting BB.

That winter I developed bronchitis. It was horrible. Every winter after that time I got bronchitis. Back then, they didn't call it COPD (Chronic Obstructive Pulmonary Disease). It continued into my mid-twenties. In the latter years, I suffered with bouts of bronchiectasis.

Every year, my cough would get worse and my medical doctor would prescribe stronger medicine than the year before. Every year, the disease got stronger and my body got weaker. It occurred to me that I was probably going to die young.

But I wasn't ready to die. I didn't know who I was yet, or what I wanted to do with my life. I was afraid, yet I had this inner feeling that prompted me to search for answers. It quickly evolved into a passionate drive. I was desperate.

One of my clients suggested that I read *The Seven Spiritual Laws of Success*. I cried as I read the book and realized that I had suppressed my ever-evolving spiritual beliefs my entire life. As a child sitting in church, I hadn't been able to make sense of some concepts, but whenever I'd questioned them, I'd gotten shushed. I now realized that those feelings and beliefs were universal truths that connected me to my soul. And I discovered that I wasn't alone. The book helped me set myself free.

When I went back to the bookstore wanting to see what else Chopra had written, I was shocked to see a book called *Perfect Health*. How was such a thing possible? I had been sick all of my life. Still, I couldn't resist the urge to buy the book. As I read it, I was astonished to discover that dis-ease was something that you "got"—and that if you could "get" it, you could "un-get" it. This simple realization changed my life. I began to practice the strategies of Ayurveda, and in three months, I was free of COPD.

Wanting to learn as much as possible, I became an Ayurvedic Practitioner. At first, I tried to simultaneously maintain my grueling travel schedule as a corporate professional–having grown up in near poverty, I was proud that I had worked hard, paid my way through college, and landed a job with a comfortable salary and company car. But the struggle between my passion for what I wanted to do and the pain of what I *was* doing was tearing me apart. I resigned.

At this same time, a number of my friends developed severe health problems. One found out that she had cancer and wanted my help, but because I was still in school studying Ayurveda, I thought I was totally unprepared for her. When I went to my teacher and mentor, DeAnna Batdorff, to ask her to take on my friend as a client and let me be the apprentice, she simply said,

"She wouldn't have come to you for help if you weren't ready. You have been studying Ayurveda for many years now. You are only in my school to get a piece of paper to make you feel better. You already know what to do." I was terrified to go it alone, but I began to work with my friend, and in less than eighteen months she got exactly what she wanted: she healed herself of cancer with no radiation, chemotherapy or other drugs. I realized that I'd had to go through this experience because I had to recognize and acknowledge the POWER of innate spiritual intelligence.

I studied Naturopathy next and became a Naturopathic Doctor. I found that Naturopathy helped me fill in the gaps and corrected flaws of other holistic healing modalities I studied. I became a massage therapist because of my experience with Ayurveda and was then led to Reiki, eventually becoming a Reiki Master. However, I kept putting off doing something that DeAnna highly recommended. She said that even though I healed my body, I still breathed like an asthmatic person. She said that I had to study and teach something called Qigong.

By that time, I had studied so many modalities that I had no interest in learning anything else. In response to my resistance, DeAnna suggested that I would not really understand Qigong until I could teach it; I needed to have that level of mastery to completely heal myself. When I finally decided to investigate Qigong, I couldn't find a style that appealed to me. It wasn't until ten years later that I discovered a style of Qigong that resonated with me because the founder, Jeff Primack, was a fusionist like me. He combined breathology and many techniques he'd learned from a wide array of Qigong masters into the Qigong form he developed. This fusion was very similar to the way I developed my platform for Radiant Health Strategies. Qigong helped me to activate and empower myself in more direct ways than the other modalities that I had studied and practiced, and it was the gravity that held the other forms and modalities together for me.

Fusing the best strategies of Naturopathy, Ayurveda, Reiki, and Qigong led me to empowerment beyond anything I could have imagined, and I'm just getting started. I'm really excited about my ever-evolving empowered journey.

I started connecting with my feminine power when I began to let go of fear and stopped suppressing my true voice. I had learned how to suppress my emotions when I was a child. By the time I was an adult, it was such a part of me that it became a part of my identity. As I deepened my studies, I explored our emotional centers called the chakras. I learned that the emotions can get trapped in organs and that the lungs were the seat of guilt and grief, which is why of all dis-eases, I developed bronchitis. I learned that healing the physical ailment was just part of the journey. I had to forgive the boy who raped BB. I also had to forgive myself for losing my voice and not being able to speak up for her or for myself. I had to go back and revisit all of my childhood traumas with adult eyes.

I also had to heal and evolve my mind, my emotions, and my spirit. I had a lot of work to do, as there were many blockages to clear. Furthermore, I was heavily into my male energy throughout my young adult life as I pushed and pushed to become a successful corporate professional. I had trained myself to be a Type A personality with major control issues. But what was it to be powerful and in my true feminine self? I had no idea how to answer that question. I grew up watching some of the women of my family being abused by men or staying in substandard relationships because they didn't have the money or resources to leave. I promised myself that I would never allow myself to be put in that position. Later, I realized that this promise had kept me from allowing people, especially men, from getting close to me.

My feminine power emerged as I began to face the distorted negative emotions and fears that I had suppressed for many years and let them go. It was a process that occurred over time and is still happening. Transformation comes from letting go of all that no longer serves you. We are always evolving, growing, and becoming, as one of my favorite spiritual teachers, Dr. Michael Beckwith, would say, "Always more and never less than our true selves."

There is a process that led me to the emergence and strengthening of my feminine power. I fuse this process into every Qigong and meditation class that I teach. I always close the practice by asking participants to place their hands in a prayer position and place their palms between their eyebrows. From here, we remind ourselves to heighten our awareness, to wake up, and to see things as they really are because our energy follows our awareness. We lower our palms in front of our mouth, reminding ourselves to speak our truth, even if it causes discomfort to others. In this way, we honor ourselves first. Then we lower our palms in front of our heart, the place from which we speak and live. I will always be both teacher and student, and every time I go through this process, I educe and strengthen my feminine power.

How I Define Power

Rather than defining power in a simple or linear way, I prefer to focus on *empowerment* because my life and practice is devoted to self-empowerment. It is the foundation of all that I do. To empower means to make stronger in a wholistic way. It includes but then goes beyond the mind, body, emotions, and spirit into the unknown. How does one define the unknown? For the sake of simplicity, let me give you a practical example. I teach Qigong several times a week. From time to time, I will have very muscular students come into my class. They look really powerful and strong. However, they really struggle in my class because while they have worked hard to develop muscular strength, they have little or no muscular endurance. You cannot really call yourself strong if you do not have both strength and endurance, and to be powerful you need even more than that. So most people tend to think of power in the same way that a body builder thinks of muscular strength. However, I do not.

Power is in patience, tenacity, strength, forgiveness, reflection, endurance, perseverance, surrender, breath, and movement. It resides in a place that is called "no mind," which is not the same as not thinking. Thoughts exist in "no mind," but the focus is on the present moment. It is what Eckhart Tolle would call "the now," and what many people call "the zone." True power comes from our willingness to enter into the present moment and stay there, make decisions there, and live there as long as possible. So power and empowerment are interesting. They involve both building up and letting go, moving forward and surrendering, but not in the way most people have come to understanding surrendering. Surrendering is extremely powerful when you surrender to your true self—your soul. This is why I love what the yin-yang symbol represents. There are no absolutes, but instead a constant flow and a romantic integration of opposites.

What Makes a Woman Powerful

A powerful woman is a woman who is deeply connected to her true self. Issues of the body, mind, emotions, and spirit are deeply interconnected. She is indifferent to the influences of the outside world and doesn't allow herself to be seduced into the vortex of:

- Competing with men—women and men have different types of power and when in their true power, they enhance each other

- Comparing herself to others

- Passive-aggressive behavior

- Believing that beauty, money, possessions or social status will make her happy

- Second guessing empowering decisions that she made from her soul, even if those decisions may not be well received by others

- Devaluing or downplaying her gifts and talents

She loves and accepts herself exactly as she is. She speaks her truth with love and has a daily practice of:

- Actively listening and surrendering to her true self, i.e., through meditation

- Offering her gifts and talents to the world

- Growing, evolving, and transforming

Tools for Connecting to Your Feminine Power

I offer Radiant Health Strategies. My protocol is to look at every area of life and bring it into balance. The first area is emotions. Doing meditations that help to balance the chakras is essential for women. I also consider Qigong to be essential because in the Qigong practice, you have to slow down enough to access your true self. This is one of the reasons why Qigong is not as well known, even though it is over 5,000 years old and gave birth to many popular forms and modalities such as Tai Chi, acupuncture and the martial arts.

My protocol also involves therapeutic nutrition. This is a soapbox subject for me because there is so much misinformation out there about nutrition. What is taught in colleges, universities, and trade schools to those hoping to become dietitians or nutritionists has very little to do with food as healing. For this reason, most people who think they are eating "healthy" are not. All of my clients tell me that they eat healthy, but then they rattle off a long list of dis-eases. It's very difficult for them to accept at first that they are misinformed. For this reason, my consultations are very comprehensive because I have to "detox" what my clients think they know to be true before revealing the actual information. Power is love. Love is power. If you say you love yourself but eat unhealthy food, you have some work to do. If you run to food or alcohol whenever an emotional crisis occurs, you have not yet understood what it is to truly love the self. Power also comes from honoring the body by giving the body what it needs so that it can heal itself.

I also work with herbs through cooking with herbs, infusing herbs, and aromatherapy. Herbs have healing powers on many levels. Simply the aroma of certain herbs help to strengthen areas of the body, balance the emotions, and enliven the spirit.

Finally movement is an important tool. No stagnant person will remain healthy or powerful. There has to be movement to bring in new energy and nutrients and release old toxins. Specific movements to stimulate the lymphatic system, increase synovial fluid in the joints, stretch the muscles, and circulate oxygen and Qi (energy) throughout the body are essential. I have several versions of these movement tools on my radianthealthstrat YouTube channel as well (direct link: *http://www.bit.ly/jthealth*).

I have developed many strategies throughout my day to help keep me grounded and centered. You must decide that you will engage in self-care. There is no power in running yourself down. Here is an example of what I do. In the morning, before I get out of bed, I feel the energy called "Qi" and have a short guided meditation queued up on my mobile phone or other device. If I feel like being in silent meditation, I silently meditate, but if I feel distracted, I immediately go for the guided meditation, which can be anywhere from five to fifteen minutes. If I have more time, I take more time (i.e., do a full Qigong practice), but I make sure that I take some time to feel the Qi and meditate, even if it is just one minute or thirty seconds. I make sure to invest a few moments in silence before starting my day. I also take at least a few moments to feel the energy in the air (Qi). This connects me with the present moment. Then, as I have a few apps from some of my favorite spiritual teachers, I get a quote from them each day on my mobile phone. Even if I get busy, I'll see their little picture in my phone until I open up the app and read the quote.

Throughout my day, I listen to my body's most basic needs. In Ayurveda, we are taught to never suppress the thirteen bodily urges. So if I have to sneeze, I sneeze. If I am hungry, I grab a snack. If I have to go to the bathroom, I go immediately, even if I must excuse myself from an important meeting.

If I have been sitting for too long, I get up and stretch my hamstrings (back of thigh) and pectoral (chest) muscles. If I have time, I will do more, but I make a point of getting oxygen and increasing circulation to the muscles that have been in stagnation.

Whenever I feel stress, I inhale instead of exhaling forcefully (i.e., sighing). When you inhale, you infuse your body with oxygen at the very moment that oxygen is needed, which helps you diffuse stress in the moment.

Before I leave work, I let go of the day. If I find that I'm still thinking of a problem at work, then I will do a cleansing movement from Reiki, Qigong, or a breathing strategy to let it go so that I do not bring a distracted self home to loved ones. Again, I have examples of some of these strategies on my radianthealthstrat YouTube channel that anyone can practice at any time (direct link: *www.bit.ly/rbreath*).

In my meditation, I make it a habit to ask myself questions that came from both Dr. Karenga (founder of Kwanzaa) and Deepak Chopra:

- Who am I?
- Am I really who I am?
- Am I all I ought to be?
- Who's asking the question?

If you really sit with these questions and stay open for the answers, it will be impossible to stay disconnected from your soul, where your true power resides.

Our New Role as Women and Our Challenges

Our new role as women is to be women and not try to be men. A man's power has nothing to do with a woman's power. In fact, when a man is in his true power and a woman is in her true power, they empower each other in delicious, beautiful ways. There is no competition because they operate differently. We have to learn how to stand in our true feminine power. It is the only way to heal ourselves and strengthen our relationships. I have outlined so many ways to accomplish this, such as emotional balance, empowerment, and connecting with our true selves. The answer is not complicated. The difficulty comes in accepting the answer in its simplicity and acting on it continually as a way of life. I constantly remind people that life is like a garden: pull the weeds and plant the seeds. This is not complicated, but it is sometimes hard because we don't always "feel" like pulling the weeds. We'd rather watch TV or have a drink with friends instead. That will be OK for a short while, but weeds left to run amuck will very soon choke out the life of your precious garden.

Modern women's biggest challenges are that we don't know who we are, we can't hear our true voices, and we keep looking outside ourselves for the answer. My favorite musician, Rickie Byars Beckwith, has a lyric in one of her songs that says, "The way in is the way out." We keep looking further and further outside of ourselves. Is it what this celebrity or that one is doing? Celebrities are always endorsing products, but what do they really know about those products? OK, if Venus Williams endorses a tennis racket, I will listen to her, but that is probably the only way I will entertain a celebrity endorsement. Who's driving the latest car? What pair of six-inch heels can I wear to make me look "chic" at the cocktail party?

Consider this example: A corporate professional woman is pregnant. She continues to wear her high heels and drink wine because the doctor said that it is OK in moderation, and she wants to "prove" that she can do pretty much whatever she wants, even though she is pregnant. What exactly is she trying to prove? When it is time to deliver the baby, she decides that she wants the baby born on a specific date, so she has labor induced, and so that she doesn't have to do too much work, she gets a C section— along with a tummy tuck if needed. When we start to live our lives in this way, we lose connections to ourselves. Nature has a way of being, and when we go against nature, it is like jumping into the ocean and trying to swim against the current.

The answer lies within the daily practice of self-mastery and self-empowerment. You need to be the most important person that you study. When you awaken your inner wisdom, you already know all that you need to know, or you will be led directly to what you need to know. When you are empowered from the inside, you are unstoppable. However, if social status is what makes you feel powerful, what happens when the social status goes away? Are you no longer you? Some people have social status, fame, and love from people around the world, yet they are still not happy. Why did Robin Williams commit suicide? The suicide rate has been steadily increasing and seems to intensify around financially successful people. Why? Because without self-mastery and self-empowerment, you may begin to believe that your worth is determined by outside factors such as your success—and your success can be taken away at any time. Or lots of people love the idea of you or your success, but they don't connect to the real you. How can a person connect to the real you if you never reveal it? Do you see how crazy our lives have become? The insanity of it would be comical if it were not so sad. Here's the real deal: no one can take away the gifts that come from connecting with your soul, your inner peace, your innate knowledge, your love and your power. All roads lead inside.

CHAPTER 10

Jane Villar-Gehr

Jane Villar-Gehr is a Spiritual Psychologist and passionate midwife to the rebirth of the sacred feminine as writer, producer, singer-song writer, soul coach and inspirational speaker who prefers to go by the title of Spiritually Inspired Visionary. Since founding Stargate Alliance, her conscious media and film company in 2009, Jane has served as executive producer on to film projects. Secrets Of Love and A Winter Rose.

She is also the founding executive producer of the peace platform Peace Link live! and has recently launched her singing career as Kaliyani with the single called Nammu's Invocation.

You can find out more by visiting http://Kaliyanimusic.com or http://www.stargatealliance.net.

My Story and My Journey to Power

Awakening to my own power happened gradually, but I believe it began early in my childhood when from age seven through nine I tragically experienced a "fall from grace" that for a long time shaped the way I viewed life, Spirit, and the world—and that for a very long time influenced the choices I made. Engendered through sexual molestation, this "fall from grace" was a life and soul initiation; my Catholic upbringing and my Brazilian cultural influences led me, at such a tender age, to feel like I had fallen from God's favor. As I internalized it all and believed it all to be my own fault, I was overcome with guilt and the lingering belief that there was something wrong with me. I was now a sinner and, as such, was condemned to darkness, as the heavenly doors would never open for me to enter. On a subconscious level I came to believe I had become Eve, or even Lilith, incarnate.

Only much later did I come to understand that humanity walks under deep, dark collective shadows that are nothing but distortions of truth. These shadows control us—especially women—through the greatest of all fears: the fear that we are simply not good enough, or maybe even evil.

Each time we are delivered into these initiations by life, we awaken to a new reality that in its own unique way fuels our innate desire to regain our wholeness. These sometimes even life-long journeys are our soul's homework. They define us and establish a path of inquiry that is meant to lead us to our final awakening and self-empowerment. So, as I grew, I relentlessly searched for answers. Deep in my heart I knew a real and true God would see me through and take me in, so in a sense I became very deeply curious about God's nature and the architecture of Spirit, and I sought to find truth hidden in some sacred book or scripture that would deliver me back to original Source. I began writing poems and philosophical thoughts early on, as if inspired by that calling to reconnect. By fourteen, I had read the entire collection of Kahlil Gibran, a Sufi mystic. I visited many local churches and religious sects, including the Rosicrucian society, the Spiritism centers of Allan Kardec, and some Christian Rationalism. I was introduced to the abundant availability of Umbanda centers and attended their ceremonies, witnessing much trans-channeling and many psychic mediums speaking in tongues. I learned and practiced Chiromancy, Tarot, Kabbalah numerology, Hatha yoga, and energy healing. At sixteen I used to take people's pain away with magnetic passes, practiced in healing touch. All this intense search evolved until I declared my psychology major in college and got really busy with a 7 a.m. to 5 p.m. daily academic schedule at the Federal University of Rio de Janeiro(UFRJ), where my path led me to a more mental exploration of the psyche, it's many defense mechanisms, and the power of the subconscious, while I fell in and out of love with Freud. Although all these mystic musings brought me some level of relief, most of the heavy healing was to come much later on.

As time went by, I grew increasingly aware of the undercurrents that had been subliminally planted in my subconscious mind and were running my programs. This awareness allowed me, with time, patience and assistance, to liberate myself from the grip of things I'd been conditioned to believe—old fears that had limited my reach and affected my sense of self-worth. Again, these belief systems included cultural, familial, and religious customs. Altogether, they formed what I like to call the "underground operation," which influenced every choice I made.

I felt some of these fears consciously, while I experienced others on a subconscious level; they were usually reinforced by my own misinterpretations of my life experiences, which in turn, were induced by those same limiting beliefs. This feedback loop is what tends to keep us stuck in the fear maze, and many times it can only be broken when the wear and tear brings us down to our knees. In those moments of complete surrender under the weight of heart-opening pain, we finally let go of our illusion of control, or of our mind's conditioned sense of separation and aloneness, and we can then remember who we are as divine children. In despair, we cry out to Spirit, and a heartfelt rocket of surrender is launched onto the Universe as invitation for it to co-create with us as we awake us to greater conscious awareness. In these precious times, we are often met by some kind of divine intervention and can feel miraculously touched by Grace.

That is, in many ways, what happened to me at another potent initiation eleven years ago when my life as I knew it completely fell apart and I had to reinvent it from scratch after my fourteen-year marriage came to a sudden end. I had no extended family in the country, a broken heart and four young children to care for. Ironically, I had lost touch with my true deeply mystical nature during those years because by doing so, I thought I'd be protecting him. This is an intricate story, the details of which, for the sake of privacy, I've been asked not to share. The important point, however, is that this deeply felt sense of hopelessness was the catalyst that brought me down to my knees in prayer and woke me up to feel a sense of my true mystical essence again. Just before the tower completely crumbled, I could hear the muffled rumbling noise of the underground current of an imminent earthquake. I felt a deep calling to say every morning and night a long old prayer I'd heard as a teen in some of the Kardecist centers I used to visit. I looked it up and began my reconnecting quest through this ritual, which lasted several weeks. I can't quite remember the exact moment when it stopped, but I do remember that all of a sudden all that was hidden got revealed and my life unraveled. The quake hit, and all the pieces went flying out in a seemingly awful disarray. At the same time, however, I started feeling the presence of this powerful feminine being come to me in many different streams of manifestation, through dreams, visions, messages, and / or images. The powerful and simple ways in which this being showed up in my life many times brought me to tears. I surrendered while in the mystery of it all and was flooded by an immense feeling of gratitude and a deep sense that even though I thought I would have to go through this alone, I was not alone at all and that in truth I had friends in very high places! Soon enough, I was surrounded by the most amazing support group, friends that I didn't even know I had, and I fell in deep and soulful love. In the midst of one of the most sad and most scary transformational moments of my life, I found myself feeling blessed and paradoxically in a continual state of bliss and deep gratitude. I felt unmistakably touched by grace.

My definition of grace is that it is a peak experience, one not induced by psychedelics, meditation trance, or any other catalyst. It is a product of the pure interaction between life and the Mystery. By definition, a peak experience is a high point in the life of a self-actualizer, during which the person feels ecstatic and more alive and whole than usual. It is a spontaneous event or series of seemingly unpredictable events—one that usually leaves us with a marked sense of having experienced the sacred. My life has been blessed and reshaped by it.

I feel that some people confuse enlightenment with peak experiences or Grace. I keep those in their respective places. A peak experience can have in itself enough power to change one's perspective in life and carry one forth with a sense of inspiration that may from that moment on guide us each step of the way. However, to me, enlightenment is a continuous evolutionary unfolding towards infinite wisdom…to me this process never ends, and its greatest catalyst is something we call "Life."

My journey to power is a continuum that's ever evolving, yet I'm able to look back from this point and see the places in this continuum when I was born again from the sacred marriage of life and grace and came to be ever more in tune with my power and divine nature. Each life initiation has asked me to step into my courage with much greater passion and confidence, so I could get to experience the fullness of who I truly am—to know myself anew, each time wiser, more empowered, more compassionate and more forgiving. Most importantly, over time my concept of the divine underwent some very necessary reframing, which was a crucial part of the healing process for me as I grew stronger and unafraid to question the "hand-me-down" concepts of reality that no longer served me.

I'm not as interested in any of the story lines and details of these initiations, as there are many of them and at the same time, they're all universal. They're all archetypal or stereotypical stories of initiations inserted within different individual lives, each with their unique flavor, and most, if not all, of us get to experience some form of them at one time or another. We can all remember and even classify a few of them, regardless of whether we have personally experienced them. Some examples include tales of betrayal, guilt, loss, rape, separation, molestation, shame, slavery and violence. Sometimes we experience the psychological aspects of these without the physical, and sometimes both. A few of them can be experienced concurrently. These initiations can vary also in degree of intensity and duration, yet what's most significant about these experiences is not their intricately unique nuances, but how present we were during them and what we harvested from them afterward. The sun may set each day, and yet we can only remember the unique wonder of a few sunsets at which we were present—the way the sun evanesced in a prism of warm rays as we stood witness, holding our gaze into that horizon and choosing to seize that moment with all of our being.

How true to ourselves were we? How deeply did we surrender to that higher call to step with courage into the unknown and trust? How much less afraid of the "dark" have we become? Were we able to capture the inherent invitation from the Universe to allow it to come and co-create with us? Or were we so deeply consumed by our victim mode and too rooted in our fears to hear anything but the rumbling of our own mind chatter? If the latter is our truth—and most of us, if not all of us, have been there at one time or another—you can be assured the same lesson will come around again and we'll go back to try again until we get it. I certainly have. There's nothing wrong with it, as this is to me the soul's homework of this earth school!

What we aim, in our daily inner search, to accomplish by reading, reaching out to our friends, praying, writing, or meditating is to gain greater understanding of this process so we can figure out the shortest cut to learning and not have to recycle these lessons again. I strongly believe that learning to overcome our fears, learning to know, accept, and love ourselves fully, and learning to express our authentic truth are all interrelated and hold the key to a new level of liberation fundamental to our sense of fulfillment. None of it is a short fix; it is an ongoing practice, with life, the ultimate mystery school, as primary teacher.

With every new level of awakening, we'll experience an ever-growing sense of our own magnetism and the ability to manifest our heart's desires in ways that at times will seem nothing short than a miracle.

We develop a sense of knowing from the beyond—a connection with a nurturing source that brings us into the knowing that all is well and that in time all is to be revealed with greater clarity.

How I Define Power

Power is a very charged word that can represent the twofold dualistic nature of this dimensional reality we dance in. In its lower frequency manifestation, power is associated with control and dominance, the more egocentric realm of that quality. I would say it has more of an electric quality, a force that pushes, manipulates, and seeks gratification. It is derived from the illusion that we are alone and separate and that, as such, we are the absolute and sole managers of our destinies, which we must at all cost control. However, true power, which sources from a higher frequency state, is related to magnetism, coherency, alignment, and integrity and is associated with the most powerful force in the Universe, which we call Love. Power, to me, is defined as our capacity to magnetize a field into manifestation, which happens when we vibrate in that highest frequency of the unifying field of love—not a limited personal/relational love, but a more embodied, full-spectrum presence that is in touch with the core essence of being and recognizes the oneness, interrelatedness, and interdependence of all beings. This love is trans-conceptual and is actualized as compassion, sacred action, sacred activism, and generosity.

What Makes a Woman Powerful

What makes a woman powerful is her depth of connection with her higher Self and how much that connection is sourced from her deep self-acceptance and self-love. The more a woman knows herself, the more embodied she becomes in her confidence, inherent wisdom, and magnetism. A woman in touch with herself is like a living flame of inextinguishable light and heat; like the sun, she lights and warms up the world and all beings around her.

My favorite way to describe what makes an empowered woman is through the tantric Hinduistic philosophy definition of Shakti. Shakti is the universal principle of energy, power, and creativity. It is the primordial cosmic energy permeating the universe and all dynamic forces active in it. A Shakti woman, thus, is the embodiment of the divine feminine, and just as Shakti is known to exist in a state of complete independence, known as svatantrya, while interdependently connected with the entire universe, so is a Shakti woman capable of feeling her deep interconnectedness while being aware of her cosmic interdependence and creative power.

In a woman in her full power, there's an increased sense of trust and a tendency to flow with and resist less. Her sense of duality, or separation, is strongly diminished, and she experiences a sense of her innate freedom of action, choice, and power that comes from a sense of intimacy with Source and with herself and from the recognition of her being an extension of that Source.

Tools for Connecting to Your Feminine Power

It's accepted in tantric philosophy that the macrocosm is nothing but a reflection of the microcosm and vice-versa, meaning outer reality is a reflection of our inner reality. Connecting to our feminine power requires deep work in sorting what is truly ours from what has been impinged upon you, programmed into you, or vicariously absorbed by you from your familial, cultural, or religious imprints.

A willingness to step into our courage is paramount so we can face those aspects of us that are out of alignment or integrity and create confusion and incoherence, mentally as well as emotionally. These misalignments, when unresolved for extended periods, can be a serious disservice to our health in the future. Blocked energy and static in the energy flow often create a lack of resonance with the things we most desire to attract for ourselves. We need to look with fierce determination at our lives and the choices we make to uncover, undo, and rebuild it from a place of clarity, consciousness, and authentic presence.

It surely sounds easier said than done, and when we are ready for the transformation the "r-Evolution" begins. Sometimes the winds of change must sweep us off ground, like Dorothy before we can land in Oz, so we can consciously find our way back home again or realize that we never really left. Oz is but a state of being, and the tornado is simply a hand from the Universe rearranging the pieces for your own highest good and quickest evolution.

What's important to take to heart is that when we start to climb a mountain, it is impossible to see what is on the other side, and sometimes that creates doubt and fear and discouragement.

The way I keep track of my vision of the other side of the mountain and feel reassured of my steps and direction is by checking my inner alignment with my choice to move forward. How strongly do I feel about that choice, and most importantly, what is it that is motivating, feeding, and fueling it? Is it coming from a place of integrity and alignment with my innermost values? Or is it coming from an egotist, self-serving, or incoherent and confused place? When the latter is the feeling I get, I then know the result will reflect that same incoherent state, so I must continue to work to find the proper alignment or a different path. However, if I feel clear and aligned with my innermost values and virtues that I wish to cultivate, my courage to continue is fueled. It's important to remember that courage is not the absence of fear, but the ability to move past it and see beyond it to the treasures waiting on the other side. Courage beyond fear is a sign that we are tapping into our inherent wisdom and breaking through our past limitations. Once our heart strength is revealed, the next stage of connecting with our feminine power is simply to exercise it consciously and from that place serve as an example for others to join in this reawakening of their own heart-minds and join the march in this global "Luvolution."

So far, what I've just described was a neutral or seemingly genderless process that both man and women would need to cultivate before they could muster the necessary heart presence to become connected and awaken to their primordial feminine, their true shakti nature. For thousands of years history with the "powers that be" have neglected and oppressed those values deemed as feminine—and especially women, the more natural containers of these qualities, have overcompensated through the women's liberation movement by becoming hardened or "masculinized."

As the result of eons of a patriarchal establishment that promoted oppression over freedom, aggression over communication, fear over love, competition over collaboration, detachment over connectedness, wastefulness over sustainability, greed over equality, arrogance over humility, abandonment over nurturance, death over birth, and war over peace, we were brainwashed to believe that all things associated with being feminine were less-than or weak and undesirable. Now, as we stand in the edge of the precipice and realize a radical shift is in dire demand, we've come far enough to be able to look back and learn from our mistakes. We are right now, in this moment in history, facing a transforming realization—that we must restore ourselves to wholeness and restore our true natures as balanced beings, in equal parts of yin and yang, or we will perish. This rising awareness has prompted our current experiencing of a profound renascence of those once rejected values, and now the time has come for inner and outer recognition and restoration of the sacred in the feminine.

Our New Role as Women and Our Challenges

One of our main roles as women is to lead by example in restoring ourselves to wholeness because we are naturally, and particularly in this moment in time, capable of much less rigidity than our male counterparts. We have for the longest time danced between the play of female and male archetypes with a relative level of comfort. We have been more flexible in our cultural behavior, fashion, and work choices, navigating both worlds. We grew to learn to adapt to and taste from it all with a natural sense of ease. However, the struggles we have endured in order to experience this level of freedom we do today are not to be underestimated or forgotten, as we now stand on the shoulders of many passionate women who have risked their lives and suffered abuse, humiliation, imprisonment, and death in order to conquer for us this level of sovereignty, which most of us happily and rightly often feel morally obliged to maintain. We must start with the woman in the mirror, doing the inner work of clearing the confusion and the overcompensating parts of ourselves that are still acting from programming and overreacting. I don't mean unlearning our positive "masculine" aspects, but checking them continually for calibration and balancing. This requires years and even a lifetime of small changes, so do not feel discouraged. As Lao Tzu's saying goes, "Knowing others is wisdom, knowing oneself is enlightenment." Concurrently, we have to take the even harder step, for some, of rebalancing into wholeness, which means to wholeheartedly re-embrace our femininity, our softness, our magnetism, our nurturing ability, and our compassionate heart— in sum, to awaken in us the power to love beyond measure, unafraid, unbound, and unrestricted. Though this openness renders us susceptible to more pain, having our hearts open, free, and available to feel all there is to feel is the key to our magnetism, aliveness, and connection with source intelligence. As the mystic poet and prophet Khalil Gibran wrote in *The Prophet*: *"But if in your fear you would seek only love's peace and love's pleasure, Then it is better for you that you cover your nakedness and pass out of love's threshing-floor, Into the seasonless world where you shall laugh, but not all of your laughter, and weep, but not all of your tears. Love gives naught but itself and takes naught but from itself."*

One challenge for women is that it's easy to lose themselves in their work, their marriage, or their kids, and they forget about themselves. We, as women, have undergone millennia of oppression and "spiritual" rejection, and many times—through the violent enforcement of the rich and well-established religious agenda—women were contained, controlled, and exploited. The most basic foundational example in our western culture lies in our biblical creation myth, which blames Eve, the primordial woman, for the entire fall of humanity.

Clearly, after eons of being held at best as second class, and many times as impure and evil, women have a shattered sense of self-worth. No wonder that so many of us start out with a sense of disempowerment, unaware of why it feels so hard to be in the world. It doesn't matter if we have been conscious of these imprints or not; they have impregnated "the air we breathe" and permeated our being subliminally along the way, exercising their deleterious influence as we went along. The lingering sense of fear, guilt, and shame, which seem to have been our common companions growing up, are, to me, largely responsible for our unwillingness to express our truth and trust our own voices. Regardless of what women have conquered in the last one hundred years, the cellular memory of this enduring negative "bashing" and the fear-laden compliance on our part in order to preserve our lives or safety is deeply engrained in our psyches.

To survive, women sought constant approval and acceptance, as would most humans when trying to make it through any type of enslavement. As a result, it conditioned us to seek value and approval from outside ourselves. The constant need to be doing, working, and pursuing perfectionism has been the palliative of choice amongst us for soothing the pain caused by that underlying perception. The absence of inspiring female role models, for instance in our school-taught history, combined with misogynous signals disseminated in our society and culture, helped these feelings of disempowerment continue to grow. Even though in many countries around our world we can still witness pervasive oppression and subjugation of women who are enmeshed in a cultural-religious-political regime that counters their efforts to create change, in some many other countries we have for the first time been able to observe new more positive models of relating becoming available for future generations.

Increasing our awareness of these historic precursors is, to me, a great first step toward liberation and the beginning of change. We can't stop the bleeding unless we know where the wound is, and we can't stop the wounding unless we know what inflicts it. This isn't to say that all personal sense of lack of self-worth or "not-good-enough" comes solely from our historical legacy, but it sure plays a definite part that is collectively and archetypically shared among all women. I, like so many of us, have had to patiently grow out of my own limited perceptions to come out where I stand today, and the process was twofold, initially on the personal level and progressively awakening to those wounded aspects that come from the collective scars all of us share. Being aware of which triggers are real and which ones are projections of aspects of us we have not yet accepted, or are rooted in cellular memory or trauma, are fundamental discernments. It's also crucial to realize that there's no use being upset at ghosts of the past. In short, I choose to see some of those lingering old-paradigm-based responses still present in our time as simply unawake and thus in some way as innocent as an unborn fetus in the womb would be.

That brings us to the next crucial point: that with awareness comes great responsibility. I believe our most important role at this time is to inspire others to rebirth themselves, to wake up, especially those who are stuck in fear or rigidity as a result of our collective past imprints, men and women alike. However, in order to do it right and not end up swinging the pendulum all the way back to another extreme, we need to wake ourselves first. For me, this rebirthing and awakening cannot be achieved in its fullness without our finding a connection to our spiritual essence. I feel it is not only fundamental, but makes the journey a lot easier when we uncover the link to our connection with the sacred, whatever shape, form, or name you may find it in. Find the link to something that inspires you to cultivate greater sense of intimacy with a much greater reality, dimension, or governing intelligence that pervades all of life. This connection, in combination with your deep desire to affect change in the world, is to me the lock and key to inner and outer transformation, which Andrew Harvey has so brilliantly and masterfully addressed in his book, *The Hope*. In this book, he coined this level of conscious action as Sacred Activism: *"A spirituality that is only private and self-absorbed, one devoid of an authentic political and social consciousness, does little to halt the suicidal juggernaut of history. On the other hand, an activism that is not purified by profound spiritual and psychological self-awareness and rooted in divine truth, wisdom, and compassion will only perpetuate the problem it is trying to solve, however righteous its intentions. When, however, the deepest and most grounded spiritual vision is married to a practical and pragmatic drive to transform all existing political, economic, and social institutions, a holy force—the power of wisdom and love in action—is born. This force I define as Sacred Activism."*

Sacred activism combines the compassionate wisdom of the awakened heart with the intelligent awareness of the necessary changes that need to happen in our collective consciousness in order for us to enter a greater level of inner and outer realities that will foster a most harmonic existence and more accelerated, while peaceful and sustainable, synergistic evolution. Combined, these two will prevent much unnecessary delay, backlash, and potential failure that many times come as a result of activism that lacks a more mature and all-encompassing vision. This vision exists beyond our small-self identity that tends to take it all so personally and resort to the old knee-jerk approach, fueled by misdirected anger, as opposed to what I like to call "fierce love." "Fierce Love" is enlightened anger, illuminated frustration, awakened righteousness. It's an elevated view of life and circumstance that allows room for a level playing field for all of us and that is awakened by the power of compassion, the greatest and most powerful force in the universe and our portal of connection to the sacred.

I believe one of women's greatest challenges is to find their point of connection with the sacred in a world where much of what has been deemed as such has not only had a strong and rigid masculine-based identity, but has also profoundly limited their sovereign direct access into experiencing and transmitting the Divine. In essence, we are dealing with a mainstream religious culture that has paradoxically promoted judgment and separation, as opposed to a truly divine consciousness, which is all embracing, inclusive, and unconditionally loving. The neo-pagan resurgence since the sixties, I believe, has been a natural progressive attempt to rediscover new ways to relate to Source as we slowly but surely have grown aware of the blatantly unconscious dogmas of our established world religions. The revival of the ancient Goddess cult is also a natural impulse and attempt to create alternative sources of inspiration and places of sacred devotional practice that offer women full access to go as deep as they wish, without any limitation. Even though I don't necessarily believe in reliving the past, I do strongly believe these were necessary and important inspirational steps in this process. I also believe we should continue to explore and find our places in whatever nouveau sacred place will honor and receive us fully, offering us alternative and more fitting forms of expression for our relationship with the sacred. I foresee a time when current religious institutions will undergo profound transformation and some will fall from the face of this planet as new alternative spiritual templates will become abundantly available. These new templates will be rich with concepts around the sacred in the feminine and offer women full access and freedom to explore their mystic nature in a much more supportive environment. Many will strive to provide a more partnership-oriented view of the sacred, where we will thrive as a collaborative society with exalted gender differences.

In the meantime, women should strive to consciously look for or create these places. Even though they are not yet abundant or fully established, we are already seeing many prototypes of these concepts becoming available for women to explore and get involved in. For example, sacred women's circles have for a while been a blessing in my own life—so much so that I decided to offer the space and facilitate one myself, as I realized how profoundly needed and deeply transforming this new sacred template can be. This act in itself served three clear purposes. First, it was an initiation for me, as with it I reclaimed my own divine authority. Second, by doing so I healed deep levels of that wound within me. And last, it fulfilled a deep yearning in my immediate circle by offering the same opportunity for other women to connect to their own inherent inner divinity, freeing them from the imprints of original sin and delivering them to the truth of their original innocence.

Through my life long personal and mystical journeying, I have traced the "original sin", Eve's "fall from grace" and the subsequent religious agenda that sought to systematically, over thousands of years, subjugate, control, spiritually reject, and through fear dis-empower females, as the root-cause of women's personal struggles permeating all dimensions, markedly the search for self-worth outside of self, an unattainable feat, when we were made believed we were originally flawed. This skewed perception, in turn, has impacted all levels of our socio-cultural functioning as humans and fostered this great imbalance of the yin-yang, which now devastates our society, nature and threatens our very potential to continue to exist and thrive as a race. For this reason I believe every women, in their own unique form must find a way to reclaim their divine sovereignty, authority and innocence and feel it permeate and heal every cell of their being, and in doing so, the collective consciousness of the universal feminine principal, the archetypal divine feminine will rebirth anew as an equally honored and sacred aspect, finally enabling us all to share balanced harmony, wholeness and oneness in every dimension of being.

CHAPTER 11

Claudia Crawley

Founder of Winning Pathways Coaching, Claudia is an executive coach and life coach for professional women over 40 seeking higher performance and new direction professionally and personally. Co-author of best-seller, Winning in Life and Work, she's currently on a mission to help women over 40, who are stuck in their careers and often overlooked, but know they have more to contribute, to create a personalised pathway up the organisational ladder.

Claudia is a mentor of women entrepreneurs internationally for the Cherie Blair Foundation programme and creator of the Page 1 Woman™. These are phenomenal women, influential self-leaders who achieve great things using their skills, experience, knowledge and talents rather than their looks. And Claudia aims to inspire and raise awareness of this 'hidden' group of leaders by blogging about their journey to leadership. Her passion for gender equality and female empowerment shines through her work.

For more about Claudia, go to www.winningpathwayscoaching.com.

My Story and My Journey To Power

*"I am grateful to be a woman. I must have
done something great in another life."*
- MAYA ANGELOU

I was born in Jamaica. When I was three weeks old, my father, like many Caribbean people at the time, moved to England. When I was nine months old, my mother made the same trip, leaving me and my two-and-a-half-year-old brother in the care of my maternal grandmother. When I was four, I stood on the tarmac of Kingston airport in Jamaica, my brother holding my hand, and boarded a plane for London, leaving my grandmother in tears behind us. Did I feel tearful on the tarmac? No. I remember feeling vexed with my grandmother, thinking she was sending me away. I thought that somehow, like my mother and father, this was because she didn't love me. So I didn't turn to wave goodbye. When we arrived in London and met my parents, they were strangers to me. And the difficult process of establishing a relationship with both, but especially with my mother, contributed to the "story" of who I was. Over the years, I created my story of a little child abandoned and unloved, a story reinforced when my mother left home and my parents got divorced when I was ten. I took that story into my adult life.

I was reminded of that story when I was about twenty-five years old and out of the blue contracted Bell's palsy, a facially disfiguring ailment. It was badly treated, and what could have been a temporary loss of movement to the right side of my face became a permanent loss. Imagine living with this condition, my disfigurement visible to all. It reinforced my self-image of being unlovable.

A key part of my story—and *who I am*—is my race. Although I was born in Jamaica, I am a Black Briton. At school, I was the only Black girl in my class and experienced what I now know to have been racism. Teachers and pupils saw us (me, my brother, and sister) as an oddity, making cruel jokes about our color (e.g., we can't tell if you're clean or dirty) and touching us without our permission. As a child, I felt demeaned but powerless to stop it. Eventually, I developed a way of both fighting back and defying the stereotype of Black people as inferior and stupid, and that was to excel at school and continue my education to university (and beyond). My journey became clear to me later. With racism a part of my social and working life, I embraced the anti-racism movement as a powerful way to identify and counter racism and other inequalities in all forms.

However, over time, what I came to take from such pivotal experiences was that we must examine feelings and perceptions to better understand them. The "story" I'd constructed (around leaving Jamaica and later when my mother left) gave me a lopsided understanding of my experiences. My journey to full understanding and healing began in earnest when I got myself a Transactional Analysis therapist and, later, a psychotherapist. When I unpacked my "story," I discovered that excelling academically was also my way of winning my mother's love. I was then able to go to my parents and find out their story. They told me that they loved me and my brother very much and had left us to create a better life for us. By the way, notice how my "story" put me at the center.

My parents themselves did not have it easy. Living in the Midlands in the 1950s and 60s, when racial discrimination was a cruel fact of everyday life, was tough for Black people. I had also minimized key counter-influences that were significant markers on my journey: going to grammar school when Black children weren't seen as clever enough to do so; having ambitious parents who expected their children to do well; gaining a place at university (at a time when only 5% of the population did so), which enabled social mobility; and having a positive attitude to hard work and public service—all of which have served me well since. I later became aware that the long-term separation of a nine-month-old child from its mother can disrupt the bond and have an enduring obstructive impact on that relationship and subsequent others. It is little wonder that I found it difficult to develop other relationships—a feature of my life that I've learned to overcome.

A key thing I learned was that however "true" my journey has been (i.e., how I construct it), it need not determine me. This was liberating. How did I learn this? Through initiating professional help. Yes, you only have to ask for such help—but first, you need to recognize that you need to ask. And the "need" that prompts such asking can change significantly. As you will see in my case, that is the journey. The discovery underneath that lesson is that if you want to be "successful," be your own impetus. And oh, my face—it didn't really matter ultimately, and it hasn't limited my life. Some people notice it and others don't. My journey, however, continues.

After graduating, I became a probation officer working with offenders. Every two years, I moved laterally in search of broader experiences and increased skills. I guess this was a sign that, far from settling, I was seeking more. A few years later, I was promoted to team manager—the first Black woman in my service to make it into management. I finally moved into Family Justice, managing social workers working with family courts. Public duty strongly influenced me. The majority of people in my profession were women working in a tough environment with warring parents and traumatized children.

As a young professional Black woman, I was also figuring out my relationship to another pillar that structured society— gender. I was brought up in a home that was very traditional— my father was head of the household. I saw how strong, capable, and talented the women in my family and my professional life were yet how male-dominated the world was—one that created greater life-chances for men. I became involved in promoting equality and diversity generally and more involved specifically in gender equality. If women were to be more powerful, there was an immense need to express it. This issue—spotting and tackling injustices such as discriminatory practices—however daunting and challenging, is one of my core values, part of my identity. Working in a female-dominated profession gave me an opportunity to experience and challenge traditional power structures and become a black feminist.

All these issues—the awareness of the need to challenge, the seeking first to understand, and the thwarting of legitimate power (let alone what it was and how other women could manifest it)—were beginning to come together when, In 2010, I was made redundant. As a defunct knowledge, learning, and professional development manager, I had to build a new identity. Fortunately, I had picked up the signs two years earlier and applied for organizational funding and trained as a coach. So despite the knock to my self-belief and self-image, I was very well prepared. When the time came, I relinquished my status as an employee and joined the scary world of business ownership.

My business, Winning Pathways Coaching, aims to enable professional women over forty to increase their work and/or personal performance. These are the sort of women I'd spent a significant part of my professional life amongst, so my skills and experience have not been wasted. As successful customers have said, it helps them to reach ambitious, challenging goals *faster*, overcome obstacles and defensiveness, and take charge of their journey. This is the power of coaching.

My Page 1 Woman™ concept is designed to counter *The Sun*'s (a UK tabloid) Page 3 Girl, who poses in nothing but her knickers each day. My Page 1 Women™ achieve great things, despite sexism, stereotypes, and objectification. They are unsung heroines, self-leaders, powerful women in their own right. They have their own working definition of success (different from the traditional "become a millionaire"), and they are working hard to achieve it. They include women like Sepi Roshan, who set up Astute Radio online to give minority women a voice; Sue Liburd, a black woman who leads a global management consultancy; Derynn Cope, who manages construction projects in a male-dominated world, and Genevieve Zawada, a serial entrepreneur. My aim is to publicize their efforts, capabilities, achievements, and the power of self-leadership, and highlight the message *"If these ordinary women can do it, so can you."* Women are so much more than sexual objects.

Alongside a monthly newsletter and regular one-to-one executive coaching and life coaching, I run workshops for women facing redundancy who need to future-face faster, managers seeking coaching skills, and, more recently, women over forty who want to scale the heights of their organizations.

How I Define Power

"What would happen if one woman told the truth
about her life? The world would split open."
- MURIEL RUKEYSER

Everybody has power in some form—for example, the power of choice, of self-leading, and making things happen. Power is one of the most democratized properties, though to be effective, we need to know what it is and how to use it. Every successful person needs to be aware of how power manifests itself. For this, she also needs an inbuilt detector to identify and counter myths around power, particularly when they apply to women. Such myths include women who "have it all," or women excelling in narrow, restricted roles that reinforce low pay and low status. Without this myth-countering ability, people, including hard-headed managers, can be gullible.

A while back, I was coaching an experienced middle manager—let's call her Mona—who felt that she was increasingly ineffective in her work. I asked her what power she felt she had. "Very little other than my title," she said. We then explored what types of power exist and came up with what is a fairly traditional list: physical, resource, status, expert, and personal. Yes, there are also others that are probably individualized versions of these. Mona was also limiting herself in a very common way: she could be more influential but *"hated the internal politics of the company"*– while mistakenly thinking she could escape company politics by ignoring it. She agreed that power is a property that exists in all organizations and that politics is the way it is enacted. So, clearly, to influence events she had to be involved. This was a breakthrough for her—she needed to spend more time with the organization's influencers to get her concerns aired and acted upon.

What Makes a Woman Powerful

The first source of power is language. So let's be clear what we mean. I am reluctant to use the term "feminine power," as to me it denotes a particular type of behavior that is stereotypically expected of women—i.e., submissive and compliant. My power is about making things happen, and it means being able to influence people. It is also about recognizing that as a Black person and a woman, I am equal to others, regardless of who they are. And knowing this, I behave accordingly. It is about being able to interact positively with people, even in conflict situations, taking a win-win approach so that my adversaries and I both benefit.

We all have personal power: it is how we use it that matters. Here are some of mine.

I have self-power, a form of self-belief. Believing in who I am and in my capabilities, I'm better able to appreciate my achievements. Then, I truly value and respect myself. When we as women value ourselves and stay true to this even when disrespected, undermined, or abused, we are holding on to our power and are better able to turn those circumstances around in our favor. We gain the respect of others.

I strive to self-lead, by which I mean that I influence myself so that I'm proactive, self-motivated and self-directed. Through self-leading, I'm better able to influence others. When things need changing, I tell myself, *"Effort is key and it's up to me."* This helps me to establish direction and act.

I have an emotional power of staying calm in a crisis. So I'm able to manage my anxiety and think clearly to avoid rash decisions. This benefits those I'm with as well as myself.

I promote equality, a theme in my professional and personal life. By acting individually and collectively to continually tackle inequalities, I aim to make the world a better place for women. So I'm standing against my oppressors rather than passively colluding with them. This is a continuous struggle that demands perseverance and persuasiveness.

What makes a woman powerful? Traditional thinking has moved on a little from the "men are aggressive and women are nurturers" approach. However, if we look at many of the characteristics attributed to powerful women, such as self-acceptance, knowing one's strengths and making the most of them, self-leading, and having an empathetic approach, it is clear that these can be learned by anyone—even men, who often do.

There is of course, however, one area of power that clearly distinguishes men from women. Produced in pain, it is often overlooked and undermined. But once created, it can never be forgotten by the woman herself. This power is so vast that it gives life and then sculpts, nurtures, and fiercely protects this life. It provides a child's first love, through which that child learns to love and be loved, and instills in a child values that feed directly into society. Such is the power of motherhood.

For any woman to express even her *ordinary power*, she must be aware that the whole "role of women" issue has been corrupted by myths, and "sound bite science," such as "Women like to talk, men prefer action" (Deborah Cameron) and myth-making that broadly reinforces traditional male power. This is a power that many intelligent, powerful women see as "place-making" or putting women in their place. Beyond reproduction, there are very few differences between men and women that can't be explained by society's and male interest imperatives. The self-help and pseudo-scientific version of this is "separate but equal," what some women critics have called gender-apartheid. While legitimate female power means "different and equal," we need to recognize that whatever differences exist between the sexes, they are overwhelmed by their similarities.

Tools for Connecting to Your Feminine Power

So how can a woman connect with her power and be the magnificent being she really is? Here are the predominant ways to do so.

Be authentic: When a woman is aware of her values—what's most important to her—she'll have a clear sense of who she is. And when she is true to herself, she'll not settle for relationships, work, or situations that make her uneasy and anxious. When we are genuine, we shine in other people's eyes.

Be a self-leader: in other words take a DIY approach. Don't wait for others, or you will wait forever. Lead yourself and make things happen for yourself.

Believe in yourself and your power to achieve. You will recognize your successes; you will see opportunities and seize them. Do not internalize the world that is hostile to women and not believe in yourself. Do not hang out with hang ups!

Take time to focus on yourself and your own well-being. You cannot be a good mother, a good employee, or a good business owner if you do not take time to nurture yourself and look after your own needs.

Maintain a positive mindset. This draws positive people toward you who help to boost your energy level. It breeds resilience and creates the staying power that's required for your journey. So avoid hanging out with negative thinkers, as they will drag you down.

Get a coach or mentor to support you and develop a support network. When you need help, encouragement, and clarity, a good coach will help you empower yourself and achieve your goal faster. You cannot be successful alone. Even Oprah has had mentors on her journey to success.

Be critical and analytical. No new ideas are built successfully without analysis first. Let us dispel the myth that analysis is the enemy of intellectual enjoyment.

Develop yourself continuously. Seek diverse development opportunities to grow constantly. In an ever-changing world, staying a step ahead by being prepared will help to open doors for you, no matter your age.

Celebrate your skills and achievements including those that come with motherhood (which are often overlooked). Publicize them at work or in your business. Show the world what you are capable of. And keep going. Remember, anything worth having is worth fighting for.

Our New Role as Women and Our Challenges

"If we are going to see real development in the world then our best investment is women."
- DESMOND TUTU

The modern-day Western woman has greater choices than her mother and grandmother did. Gone are the days of hiding her talents and intellect and living her life solely as a stay-at-home mum and a supportive wife. With these increased opportunities, she can go to university and not be part of a tiny minority. She can take her pick of a range of career options that women before her could only have dreamt about. She can have a career and family or choose one without the other. However, the experience of women in the West is not reflected worldwide. And the structures supporting gender inequality remain firmly entrenched, regardless of where in the world you live.

Despite the broadening of our horizons, many women have still not fully embraced our newfound freedom. Like men, women have been raised in a world of gender biases and expectations that favor men. So often we are brought up to be less than we actually are, and many of us continue to keep our strengths hidden and are plagued by fear and beliefs of not being good enough. Having internalized the "men are superior" mantra, many of us fail to make the most of our potential and the growth in opportunities. My friend Susan excelled in that "male subject," science. She could have done well in science-related professions but chose instead to hide her potential, get married soon after leaving school, and put the needs of her husband and children before her own. The choices were there, but she mirrored the example of the women in her family and seemed bound by the limitations they had experienced.

In addition, women often allow structures that perpetuate gender inequality to hold them back. So we tolerate the likes of unequal pay for equal work, being passed over for promotion, and economic policies that affect women more negatively than men. Within this modern-day paradox of increased choices but restricted mindsets, is there a new role for women? I would say "no," but there are roles that many more women can exploit—and in so doing, they can change the world.

The first role involves our taking responsibility and action to free ourselves from constricting beliefs, such as those that support the view that women are inferior and that maintain our individual low self-esteem. Once free of such debilitating mindsets, we are in a better position to bring about change and step into our greatness. The challenge: such beliefs may be held unconsciously. So bringing them into awareness is the first step, and replacing them with empowering beliefs follows. Working with an effective coach can help you overcome this challenge. And surrounding yourself with supportive people helps the process of your empowerment.

The second role involves the mothers amongst us making the most of their power to influence society's thinking and raising their sons and daughters as equals who should expect great things of themselves. This is a key step towards gender equality. The challenge: fathers with traditional views of male power may not give their support to raising their children in this way. And there may be counterinfluences outside the home. Getting the support of partners and the extended family is important, as it is hard teaching and role modeling gender equality alone. Being alert to other influences that children are absorbing is also key, as only then can they be challenged.

The third role involves us taking collective action and challenging the structures that perpetuate sexism and traditional male power. The UK suffragettes' victory in the early twentieth century in getting women heard and taken seriously, winning the vote, and challenging male dominance in the face of threats and imprisonment exemplifies the power of commitment, courage, and collective action. The challenge: male supremacy mindsets amongst both men and women and men's reluctance to power share could make maintaining the change momentum difficult. Nevertheless, do not leave the struggle for gender equality to others. Get involved in collective action with like-minded women—and men. You have a contribution to make, however small you might consider it—a contribution that could unleash benefits not just for women but for men too. When the pressure is removed from men to hide their "softer" side and be aggressive "real men," the world will be a better place for both genders.

The fourth role involves more of us making the most of our skills, talents, and potential, and applying for leadership roles that give us a voice at the top and the opportunity to be role models for those coming up behind us. When we are there in greater numbers, we can play a more powerful part in developing a world that truly represents the needs of both genders and thrives more on collaboration and peace and less on aggression and conflict. The challenges: balancing work alongside the role of mother requires that women are supported physically, emotionally, and financially with child care. Get your partner to take more responsibility and support you with equally shared parenting, as this is key to women's progression. These parenting roles also provide positive modeling for your sons and daughters. Collectively push your employer for appropriate parental leave and flexible working (i.e., working in a way that suits an employee's needs, like having flexible start and finish times, or working from home). And get involved in lobbying the government for improved and affordable child care provisions. Note a second challenge here—in the UK and the US, women who take time out to have children are often penalized because it is harder to get their careers back on track and get promotions. This takes us back to the second role that women can develop, that of taking collective action to challenge discrimination.

Gender equality will not be successfully tackled if left solely to men. Women have a significant part to play in bringing about change to men's perceptions and attitudes and to overcoming unconscious discrimination. We know what needs to be done more than those who maintain the structures of oppression. The world will benefit on all levels from inclusivity and making the most of talents, regardless of gender. And yes, there are women who have made it to the top already. But that doesn't mean the world has finally changed. It has not—not yet. Because it is when we are at the top that our influence in bringing about change for all women is most needed.

The power of a woman + support and collective action = equality of opportunities for both women and men.

CHAPTER 12

Carmen Paz

Carmen Paz is Mentor of hundreds of women around the world who want to shine like Spiritual Entrepreneurs. In her Private Mentoring and Programs she combines with mastery the necessary business strategies to create an effective and profitable professional practice with the spiritual wisdom needed to create a thriving business aligned to your feminine values and lifestyle. She is the founder and director of the Escuela Internacional para Emprendedoras Espirituales MUJER INICIADA™ and the creator of her Signature System The Femenine Path of ABUNDANCE™.

She is an internationally recognized author who is known by her wisdom, creativity, clarity and human simplicity that is reflected in all his work. But above all things, Carmen Paz is passionate about life and freedom at all levels and she has been actively involved in Spiritual Awakening of Women for more than 20 years.

Learn more http://www.carmenpaz.com.

My Story and My Journey to Power

My journey in life, which has been the same journey to my inner power, has always been related to my maturity as a woman. I have always been somewhat of a free and independent spirit. As a young girl, up until my teens, I used to take care of my two younger brothers, and then I married very young as well. In three years, I went from taking care of my younger brothers to becoming a full-time wife and mother, taking care of my three children. At the same time, I also had to work to earn money to help at home. Although I really enjoyed those years and seeing how my sons grew up healthy and happy, I must confess that those times were hard because my husband was not as supportive as I needed him to be. I missed the freedom to be myself, and I had to manage my life with all this pressure. In some ways I felt trapped and unable to express myself fully, so I felt that I needed to assume the masculine role in my family. Interestingly, my husband considered me a very masculine woman because I was independent, strong, and assertive. This was one of the causes of why my marriage became broken.

The driving force for me to find that powerful woman within me came after my husband and I divorced. I was being challenged in my femininity, and I felt very bad inside. After my divorce, I decided that I needed to understand what it meant to be a powerful woman in these modern times. So I embarked on an adventure of being myself, and I began to go deeper in my feminine spirituality. I chose to leave my home, and my three children stayed with my husband—though I lived quite near them and could see them every day. I had to now face my life alone after twenty years of marriage. In the beginning, it was really hard, but I must confess that at the same time it was very liberating for me. For the first time in many, many years, I was taking care of myself and I had to work for a living by myself with no help at all. However, it made me very clear about what I wanted. I started to listen to my heart again and flow with the circumstances instead of pushing the circumstances.

During my first year of living by myself, I realized that I had been pushing too hard to make things happen, acting from my masculine energy almost all the time. This was exhausting! In my new life alone, I had to learn how to go with the flow every day and face whatever the day brought. I knew that I had all the potential in me to be myself, all the possibilities in my life, but it was hard to face them. I had no plans ahead, and I just was facing every day as it came. I ended up being in a kind of recovery mode, and it took me a couple of years to recover from all these changes in my life. This was when I started to connect with my feminine power. After two years, I was able to face my feminine power and to embrace it. My feminine power was finally awakened.

During the first years of living of my own, I discovered my own inner cycles of creation, and then I decided to explore my feminine spirituality from different angles. I was aware that there was feminine spirituality around me, but I couldn't find it in the years when I was having my children and doing everything for everyone. So I decided to train as a priestess of Avalon, and I studied to be a feminist theologian. This was when I experienced what feminine energy could do for me and for the world.

It took five very intense years. I pursued the process of healing my relationship with my body, my relationship with the women in my environment, and my relationship with the cycles of life. This was the way that I could connect with my feminine power. Masculine energy is more about action, and it's not very easy for people who are in doing mode to stop and look at the cycles of life. During these years of training and living alone, it was very interesting to be able to connect with this. I discovered a beautiful way of living. In addition, the most important thing that I experienced was learning to connect with my body, the natural rhythms of life, and my inner cycles of creation. During this journey, I listened to my heart's desire and my capacity of creation, love, and compassion. All these capacities evolved in a natural way.

How I Define Power

The word "power" has several meanings. Among the definitions you will find in a dictionary, the most common is: the ability to impose control over others. Historically, power has been defined by a masculine model. The lives of women from the Iron Age until about fifty years ago, more or less, have been developed in a private sphere, while men have been doing things in the public sphere. So the feminine role in our western society has been based on what the patriarchy wanted and expected from women. Men were the ones that created the rules and decided what to do and what not to do in the world.

When women began to enter into the public world, we adapted to the established model in two ways. One way was assuming the female model that men and the patriarchal society expected from us as women. We hid our feminine power and started to use plastic surgery, fashion, attitudes, etc., to mask who we really were and just do what was expected from us as women. The goal was to be desirable and loved. I have seen this a lot with my clients and my friends. For years, women have hid their true feminine qualities in order to be accepted in the world of men on a professional level.

The goal was to prove that women were able to do things as men do and to be accepted in this world, so they hid their feminine power.

What Makes a Woman Powerful

Feminine power doesn't speak about control over things, over nature, over circumstances or people; instead it is about learning to work with the circumstances and establish a collaborative network to achieve greater wellness for all creatures on the planet. It's the power of doing things with others and not over others. Therefore, the word "power," if I look at it from my feminine point of view, is actually the capacity to work together to make this world a better place to live.

Where does this power come from? Feminine power comes from our inner realms, and what makes us powerful is the ability to develop a healthy relationship with our body, emotions, mind, and spirit. This power also comes from trusting in ourselves and knowing that we can transform our own lives. Don't listen to what we are supposed to do as women, but instead just trust in ourselves. We have the power to decide and transform our lives.

Feminine power is also the ability to create real connections with our inner biological cycles and honor them as the changed cycles of nature. This is one of the biggest secrets for women— to start honoring our inner cycles, biologically. In a masculine society, we are pushed all the time to forget that we are women, that we have our menstruation, and that we go through menopause. These things are done to make us weak. This is why it is important to embrace our power, to create a connection with our cycles and our bodies, and to learn to flow with them in our lives. I think that our power comes from a constant connection with our intuition, integrity, authenticity, and compassion and from the ability to express ourselves and share wisdom with each other with clarity and self-authority.

Tools for Connecting to Your Feminine Power

To connect to your feminine power, first stop trying to control everything and instead learn to flow under the circumstances. In addition, be open to receive abundance and let the universe surprise you. Visualize what you want to create in your life, but let the universe find how and when to bring it to you. Also, you must allow things to happen in your divine time and be patient, like a gardener does when taking care of her garden. Be willing to change and let go of what does not serve you anymore and make room for something new. This is the best tool to magnetize abundance in your life.

Another tip is to be creative and generous, and learn how to manifest your desires because they are the spirit speaking through you. You must also honor your creativity and wisdom and learn to express your feelings and emotions. This is huge because as women, we are emotional beings, but sometimes we need to learn how to express those emotions. What helps with our feminine power is to surround ourselves with images that celebrate our femininity and recover our own feminine needs, the archetypal images of the divine feminine. Make sure to heal relationships with the women in your life and be willing to share with them and not compete. These tips are some that I live by every day.

Women often like to be in control; however, I recommend not trying to have control all the time. Be open to receive, allow things to happen in their divine time, be willing to change and let go, be creative and generous, honor your creativity, surround yourself with feminine images, and be very aware of your relationship with other women.

So how do you do that? I will tell you what works for me. First, let's talk about nutrition. I try every day to see what is really good for me and not to follow nutritional advice just because others say that it's good. I think our bodies know what is better fuel for us and we have to be willing to discover what is good for us.

Another tool that works for me is to walk and dance in nature and enjoy myself doing it. Also, enter in silence with breathing and meditation—just a few minutes every day. Create a sacred space in your home to honor your divine feminine, practice everyday gratitude and generosity, and learn how to serve others in balance with your life and with them. And lastly, always be open to learn from others. Remember that we are masters of what we know, but we are pupils of what we don't know.

These tools have helped me because I have made it important to be aware of the cycles of life and honor them. This has been very helpful in my business as well. When we are in business or when we are creating a business or a project, we must always start with the mode of visualization of what we want and then we have to start putting all these ideas onto paper. I think of it like a garden. When we have prepared the soil, and the seed is ready, we plant the seed and take care of it.

The problem is that sometimes our masculine energy doesn't honor the cycles of life, because you try to see every day if the seed is sprouting. You don't leave things to grow in their own rhythm, and sometimes we push too hard. For me it was very interesting to put this in place with my business because it led me to develop a great awareness that everything has a cycle of time to manifest. When I enter in my silence and my meditation, when I create this sacred space for me in my home and I practice gratitude, I always feel in abundance and I don't feel scarcity, and it is easy for me to wait until my business or my projects or my desires go into fruition. This is one of the best tools I integrate to connect with the cycles and honor the cycles in life and business.

It becomes really easy for women to lose ourselves in our work, our marriage, or our kids. We end up putting ourselves last. When I first got divorced, my three boys lived with their father. Two of my boys are now living with me, and I have to find time for myself every day. When I was living alone, it was easier, but sometimes it's not easy when you have family and when you have to work and do everything for others. Our natural tendency is to take care of people and our home, which makes life very busy.

I have set very strong boundaries on my responsibilities and on myself. I am very aware that I must attend to certain things in my home, but there are other things that I attend to as well. So, I am very clear about my boundaries, dedicating three hours for myself every day. This time is just for me. In these three hours, I can do many things. I can go for a walk, or read, or meditate, or attend any training for myself or my business. I can also go shopping or have a massage, or watch my favorite TV show. Every day, I have these three hours for me, and my sons know that this time is for me. During this time, it doesn't matter if the dishes are dirty or the beds are undone. I don't concern myself with any of these things.

Another thing that I do is to travel for seven or more days if I can, once or twice a year. It is very important to have these types of boundaries, especially for women who are working at home, as I am, and to choose what time of the day is the best for your free time and how long it will be. It could be one hour, two hours, or three hours; it all depends on your needs. I have my office at home, and sometimes I'm working, working, working and then look up at the clock and realize I have been at the computer for three hours. Have strong boundaries and don't feel guilty about them. Just work on yourself.

Our New Role as Women and Our Challenges

I think there are two parts to the new role of women. The first one is strengthening our feminine power in all manifestations of life through our feminine values of love, compassion, connection, collaboration, service, and emotional intelligence. This is because we are women and we have a feminine body that our souls want to express in this lifetime. We have chosen to experience life through our feminine presence, and it's fundamental to honor this. In addition, feminine power has been silenced for centuries, and it needs to be restored in our lives and in our consciousness. We need to express our feminine power in all areas of life—education, science, politics, health, culture, business, and spirituality—and we must realize that the masculine model of doing things is just one face of the coin, not the only one. The feminine point of view about things is just as important as the masculine.

Once we have this feminine power in the society and in our consciousness, the second part of our new role is balancing the expressions of yin and yang forces of the universe in ourselves and in our world. We have to remember that we are whole beings and that these two universal principles have been unbalanced for many years. We are living in very important moments of change, and before we balance these two forces, we have to elevate the feminine energy in the planet and in our consciousness. Therefore, the new role of women is to discover what our feminine power is and strengthen it by finding this healthy balance.

Women are now balancing their roles as mothers and wives with being entrepreneurs or working for others, and this is not without challenges. In this process, sometimes we tend to repeat the established masculine model of doing things, a model that drains our energy. We don't have many feminine models to follow, and we don't know how to do it in a feminine way. Sometimes, too, the feminine way is not acceptable in a professional environment. So, the biggest challenge the modern woman now faces is to create a feminine model of doing things in our work, in our lives, and in our business. This feminine model must be able to serve us and to serve the community.

We must assume that this feminine model can be as useful and productive as the masculine model, and we have to be confident using it. Sometimes, women are afraid that the feminine way of doing things couldn't be as good or effective as the masculine way.

The last challenge women face in their new role is to heal our wounds around our own worth and reconcile making money and serving others without losing our spiritual values. The first step in overcoming these challenges is to make the decision to do so and have the courage to do it. When we do this, the universe receives a message that we are ready to change and ready to make the changes that we need, and it begins to bring us opportunities to do so. The next step is to be open to receiving help through a mentor, coach, therapist, or a friend who can guide us in our new role.

As I was trying to find my feminine power, I decided that I wanted to work with women. I am the founder and the director of the International School for Spiritual Women Entrepreneurs MUJER INICIADA™, where I coach and mentor women in the healing arts to create a prosperous business. I love my work; it is my purpose in life to help spiritual women entrepreneurs create a feminine business model that fits into their lifestyles and values. My philosophy is very simple: I think it's time to serve the world as spiritual entrepreneurs while we honor our feminine presence, making money doing what we most love.

CHAPTER 13

Gloria Coppola

Gloria Coppola, author, educator, health coach and massage therapist has been in the healing arts for more than 25 years. She is the former owner of a holistic health center, massage school and health food store. She is the recipient of the World Massage Hall of Fame for her dedication in the healing arts award and the Aunty Margaret Humanitarian for being the founder of a nonprofit called Massage Without Borders. Gloria currently is involved in inspiring woman around the world through education and healing retreats.

A national spiritual leader, retreat leader and grandmother, teaching is a natural environment for Gloria. She is also astudent of life. Gloria attended Clayton School of Natural Healing and obtained her health coach certificate through the Institute for Integrative Nutrition. She has studied with many icon leaders like Deepak Chopra, Carolyn Myss, Bernard Jensen, Anodea Judith, Bernie Siegal, Joan Borysenko to name a few.

She's also the author of "Both Ends of the Rainbow, A Healing Journey". Learn more at http://www.lomihealingjourney.com.

My Story and My Journey to Power

My journey in life has certainly been a long and arduous one. When I was a young child, there were always domestic situations occurring, and I was always the one stepping in to defend a sibling. My mother would stay in the living room, lacking the confidence—or perhaps the courage—to stand up to my dad. So at the tender age of five, I was the one always standing up for my brothers. I felt as if I'd come into this world with a mission to help people, especially women, who crossed my path. It was just something I knew deep inside.

I feel that inherently I've been gifted with the power to take care of, watch over, and be "mother" to other people on many, many levels. In life, I've started many different businesses and projects, learning as I went and being very successful at it. I'm the kind of girl who will get into an airplane and fly, taking out the instruction book along the way. Many people look to me for motivation, inspiration, or guidance, mainly because I do take risks in life. Sometimes I wonder, "Can I give them the right direction or provide resources for them?" I find that my experiences are usually exactly what they need to hear.

Recognizing my passion to help others has led me to owning my feminine power. I have found that I can turn around and redirect myself and put myself on another path and journey to be successful, no matter what adversity confronts me, even when I am doubtful.

I have come to realize that I'm a responder to situations— I'm like a mother when her child falls and gets hurt, running to pick her up and kiss her boo boos to make her all better. I believe that's the feminine power that I have taken into every situation, the ability to nurture and care for life. And that truly is a blessing.

Growing up to be the strong one of a family of seven and the next to last in line, I had a lot of masculine energy. I developed more of the personality that I saw in my father as I grew up. I wasn't masculine in the way I dressed, but certainly in my energy. I was a survivor! This helped me with survival skills, especially later in life as a single mom raising two kids.

I believe that we all have masculine and feminine in us. Learning how to keep them in balance is the key. Women can be a strong driving force and very powerful. This, in fact, is women's survival mechanism—it's our strength and endurance. It is our life force.

I have had many challenges in my life. Over the course of about ten years, I lost a spouse tragically, which threw me into a depression, lost my dad, lost my business through embezzlement, and lost my sense of self and purpose. I had never experienced depression before; I'd always been a happy person. This was a vulnerable phase in my life, but it was also a very powerful one. It taught me another aspect of what it means to nurture oneself. I had to run away—literally and physically leave my environment— after a year of people begging and forcing me back into a role I no longer wanted or fit into. They say wherever you go, there you are; however, I needed a change of environment and to get away from other influences. So I got on a plane and took what was supposed to be a month-long trip to Hawaii—and ended up staying there for seven years. During the first two years, I realized how out of touch I was with a lot of things. I was only nurturing certain gifts that God had given me. I was not nurturing my own life force, myself, until I took this time.

I began to get in touch with nature because nature has both masculine and feminine forces. The ocean, for example, could be very masculine and violent with turbulent waves. And yet, it could be as calm, soft, and gentle as a baby's touch. I started to look at how everything is balanced and how I had become unbalanced because of the roles I'd thought I had to play. This encouraged me to try new things like belly dancing and hula dancing. I met an Egyptian man who became a dear friend and is to this day. He taught me more about women from a cultural perspective than any woman has ever taught me. He began to share with me many things about his Egyptian culture. He commented that in the American culture women have gotten very masculine, that they have lost the identity of what being feminine really means and why we have that feminine power. He challenged me to research philosophy and go back to matriarchal societies before everything became patriarchal. The bottom line is: if we understood the power that we had as women, we could change this world.

My Egyptian friend shared with me, "You need to honor the woman part of you, the feminine part of you, and you need to be softer in many ways." At first I was insulted because I thought I was soft. He explained what he meant and suggested that I create a setting for my partner, put on my belly dancing outfit, and let the energy flow. He suggested that I make it nurturing, sensual, loving, and fun. Not sexual, but fun. He said, "Watch what happens with your relationship." And so I did.

I pushed myself out of my own comfort zone. I was skeptical, I must admit. It was interesting to also watch my partner, as he was uncomfortable with it at first. After a while he began to relax, though, and by the end we were dancing and laughing. We just lay there on the floor and held each other, and he expressed that it was wonderful to enjoy each other without any sexual expectations after a long, tiring day at work.

All these little lessons along the way have taught me not only about nurturing myself, but about what it really means to nurture someone else in a partnership. I learned that women have a power to create anything they desire, including the way we want a man to take care of and respond to us. This taught me to be able to lead powerful groups of people with respect and honor and teach others to do the same.

How I Define Power

So, what's my take on power? Power, for me, used to mean being extremely strong and determined, sometimes really aggressive and even angry. These are some of the qualities I was exposed to as a child. As a result, I didn't like power because of what I thought it represented at that time. When I began to take personal development classes, I learned that many women brought up in these environments and situations where there was a parental figure, usually a male, perceive power as violence and anger. Through my healing journey, I realized that's not what power is at all. Power is the ability to tune in to the universe in a grateful, gentle way and utilize everything that is here for us in a balanced, productive way. Power can be very productive, gentle, and strong without being aggressive. Power can be focus, manifestation, and creation. Power can be trusting oneself.

What Makes a Woman Powerful

I came to realize that power had nothing to do with what I'd thought it was when I was a young girl. I did not have to scream and yell at people to demonstrate power. Being grounded and centered and in tune, and presenting and talking in ways that were compassionate, was very powerful. So power to me became very feminine. I began to resonate with more women and became open to leaders who led by example with grace. Amazing women like Princess Diana and Mother Teresa gave to the world in a gentle way, loving themselves; they stood in the essence of who they were in all their God-given gift. That is powerful.

I've always been in some form of business, and eventually I owned a holistic healing arts center and school. I have written for many healing publications and eventually wrote a book about my healing journey. I studied nutrition, became a health coach, and owned a health food store. I even responded to an emergency crisis, which led to the creation of a non-profit organization that helped colleagues in the healing arts. All of these things, honestly, were not something that I sat down and wrote down on a goal list. These were adventures guided by my intuition. As my life continues to grow, I see everything that I've ever done came full circle. Now I find myself in a position to help people, not just on a singular basis but also on a global basis.

I receive many letters from people telling me that have been inspired by things I have written or videos I have produced or classes I have taught. I realize that in tapping into our own divine power, we can actually enhance and reach more people. I feel immense humility and gratitude to be on this planet and to be able to not only support women but also help men to get in touch with their divine feminine.

The work that I do as a health and lifestyle coach helps me to be in touch with my feminine power continually. I host retreats for women and men—training people in the healing arts and transforming lives. Right now, I'm involved in health coaching for women who want to either lose weight or get healthier. In this process, their transformations are beyond the physical. They are actually becoming more empowered and more confident about who they are as women and are realizing that it goes so far beyond just their bodies.

We identify with our body first and foremost, but once we feel well in our body, we can then tap into building confidence.

Advertising focuses so much on the physical body that many of these women have just allowed themselves to hide or to crush their gifts when they didn't feel perfect. I'm watching them learn how to take care of themselves, some for the first time. They are feeling better physically and emotionally and are spiritually more balanced. They want to do more now in other realms, and it's just a beautiful thing to watch this transformation happen. They're in love with their bodies more now, which is really super cool because so many women aren't. In loving their bodies and seeing them in a more feminine way, they are tapping into a resource they may have forgotten—a resource of self-love and of knowing they are enough!

Tools for Connecting to Your Feminine Power

If I could give women some advice on connecting with their feminine power, the first thing I would say is that it's important to be around other women—positive women. When I was going through my divorce, all the women around me were going through divorces or relationship breakups at the same time, and they were all bad-mouthing men. I pulled myself away from them. I was sad about my relationship ending, but I didn't like hearing what all these women were saying. I didn't want to be angry and miserable. I think positive support is really important. Personally, I've always been into self-development. I don't think we should ever be complacent about developing our skills and our power.

I've worked with women who have been victims of sexual abuse and were violated years ago. They needed to know that they had a safe, compassionate fellowship where they could build themselves to see their gifts. Women have a lot to accomplish on this planet. We are the caretakers of the planet, and we need to figure out for ourselves how can we do that by fully embracing and loving ourselves first.

Women often have a tendency to put others first. They get caught up in their work or their family and end up being overwhelmed and putting themselves last. I am definitely one of those women who got lost in work, in relationships, and in my kids, and I have repeated that pattern more than once. Over the years, I identified certain things, but it wasn't until about three years ago I realized I basically was addicted to taking care of everybody else but myself. I realized doing so made me unhealthy and unhappy on a core level. I finally made a decision to put myself first because otherwise I would not be good for anybody at all. Even though I'd changed over all those years of my life, I realized I was still hooked into the pattern. I was finally at a stage in my life at which I was just not willing to compromise and give up all that I had worked on. I wanted to overcome this tendency to put everybody else first.

We women need to look in the mirror and reflect, being really honest with ourselves. What are we doing, how are we contributing, and what are we teaching even our children by taking over all the time? In the last several years, I have made the decision to use the word "No" and to say "Goodbye" or "I'm done" to things, situations, people, and places that are not serving my highest purpose. After I made that decision to put myself first, lots of miracles happened. For example, I wrote my book and got it published in record time. I have listened to God guiding me to places spontaneously. My health has changed, my life has changed, and my finances have changed. There are so many things that I am now able to see more clearly because the first thing I do in the morning, after I say my gratitude prayer for being alive, is ask myself, "How do I serve and take care of me?"

In doing so, I've gained a great respect for life and my life. If you don't nurture yourself, if you don't honor the divine in you, who's going to do it?

Our New Role as Women and Our Challenges

The new role of women is essentially the old role. Women need to step up and collaborate to share our knowledge and our gifts—to help future women of this world. So many things have happened culturally in our society over the years, and I feel we're blessed to have gained many rights, but I also think we have lost some of those rights. I feel it's time for women to teach the wisdom that they know. This is what indigenous cultures have been doing for lifetimes. There's a tribe, a group of the thirteen grandmothers who travel around the world from all cultures. They have stepped up in their role to teach all of us—not only women—about the divine feminine. If we don't do this, the planet is going suffer, people are going suffer, and children—who are the future—are going suffer. We have to think about the future. As a grandmother, I wish I'd had the wisdom and knowledge that I have now when I was raising my own kids. I see things differently. I see that we are responsible for every action and every choice we make every single day because it's going to affect those grandchildren. Women, we need to be accountable for that, because we are the ones who bring them into this world. What kind of world are we leaving for them? I see women stepping up, sharing their wisdom, creating the balance, and teaching the children so they don't have to go through hardships that we may have had to endure. I believe that if we honor this wisdom, we can help make their future easier and brighter.

One of the biggest challenges for modern women is being respected *as* women. I believe that when we support each other, encourage each other, and hold each other accountable for these beautiful feminine gifts, we can accomplish much more. Women like to gather, but they don't do this much anymore. When women gather, magic happens, so we need to make that a tradition once again.

It is my wish and prayer that every woman out there respects herself. Look in the mirror in the morning and, no matter what the situation, respect yourself. You will be stronger; you will believe in yourself more. When this happens, we can get more in touch with that space in our belly where that life force lives. When that spark gets ignited and we can feel that essence of life and joy coming up through there, we can accomplish anything. We all came in this world pure, beautiful, and fully empowered. Look in the mirror and see it, believe it, achieve it. Click your heels. "You've always had the power!" The power of creation.

CHAPTER 14

Patricia Young

Patricia Young is a Certified Life & Holistic Coach, Reiki Master and Founder of Inner Prosperity Academy. After 20 years working for the Corporate World, she decided to follow her calling to help growth oriented women that are stuck in a career that is unfulfilling, but they know, deep in their heart, that there is something else they are meant to be doing. The goal of Inner Prosperity Academy is to inspire women to commit to recreating their lives to the ones they came here to live, and to give their greatness to the world. Patricia helps clients to reconnect to their Authentic Self and find their Life Purpose so they can live a more meaningful, joyful and balanced life - a life filled with Inner Prosperity, because a prosperous life begins from the inside out and it affects all areas in life. She does transformational individual coaching, online coaching programs, VIP Days, presentations and workshops. She is based in Fort Lauderdale, FL, but she serves, virtually, clients all over the world.

Learn more at http://www.InnerProsperityAcademy.com.

My Story and My Journey to Power

Living a purposeful and meaningful life not only brings joy and freedom to your life, but also creates a ripple effect in the lives of those around you and the world in general. For me, my journey to fulfillment started with unapologetic self-love and blind faith in who I was designed to be.

When I was young, I really wanted to study journalism or psychology. In Venezuela, the only option I had was to go to the city of Caracas, the capital. One day, without my parents knowing, I drove by myself to Caracas so that I could take an admissions test at the university. When I later told my parents that I had already applied and had been accepted, their reaction was not what I had expected. My dad told me there was no way he would let me go to Caracas by myself. I was only eighteen years old and a woman, which had a lot to do with my parents' decision of not supporting me. Consequently, instead of going to the university in Caracas, I stayed home in Valencia and my father paid for me to attend a private university where there were only four choices of what to study—three types of engineering, or business administration. I reluctantly chose business administration, the best of the four options for me, but not at all what I really wanted to do.

I know my parents wanted to protect me and to have me close to them—they had the best intentions. But I'm not sure if they might have reacted differently were I a boy. I'll never know because I don't have brothers, so I could never compare.

The thought of leaving my home and not letting my parents decide for me about my future did cross my mind. However, two main challenges kept coming to mind: I didn't have a place to stay or any money to pay rent and support myself. I didn't even know where to start if I decided to leave, because I had no support. I also thought of all of the suffering that I would inflict on my parents by disobeying their decision. I could feel the weight of the guilt that I would feel if I decided to leave on bad terms. Truthfully, I was also scared because I knew I would be vulnerable as a young woman in a new city with no support. I realized I was not ready to take that risk, and I ultimately decided to surrender to the idea of staying at home. Doing so meant that I had everything I needed, my environment was familiar, and I felt safe. Though I was not happy with my course of study, I had a good life and had my family close to me.

Five years later, I graduated with very good grades, but the whole process had been very tough for me because I really hadn't liked what I was studying. The next step for me was to find a job. That's when I landed my first job at a bank. Throughout all the years that went by—twenty, to be exact—I was never satisfied with the jobs I had. I faithfully did the work that was expected of me, and I was grateful for the jobs, but I couldn't get rid of the feeling of dissatisfaction and disconnection from myself. I felt I was living my life on autopilot, just going through the motions, not really living. I used to tell myself, "This can't be it. Something's missing here. There must be something else that I could do."

I spent so many hours every day at a place where I felt unfulfilled, dealing with people, situations, and an environment that were not in alignment with my values. In short, I knew I was supposed to be doing something else more meaningful, but I didn't know what it was, or even if I could get to the point of questioning the status quo in which I had been for so long already. I could just hear the people in my life saying, "Well, we all need a job. You've invested time in a career, so you might as well stick with it and work. You're earning a good living. Be grateful!"

As years went by, my feeling of disconnect continued, and I started to suffer from anxiety, lack of energy, and even some depression. Going to work was really a drag every day. My internal struggle led me to start doing some serious soul searching in order to connect with my inner wisdom and my inner power. That's when I started taking Reiki classes and massage classes ten years ago, and that's how this path led me to become a Life and Holistic Coach.

After a few more disappointments in the corporate world and the loss of two of my dear friends to cancer, I said to myself, "This nonsense has to stop. You are the only one in charge here, no one else." The loss of my friends was like a slap on my face, a wakeup call. It made me realize that I didn't want to look back to my life one day and see that I hadn't given myself the opportunity to do what I loved. I didn't want to regret that I hadn't had the courage to live a meaningful life.

I took responsibility, reclaimed my power, and said to myself, "This is my life, and I need to act and take responsibility. It doesn't matter what others could or would say because I need to start taking actions to live the life that I came here to live." So I chose to take action to make my own path. I had been following the path of convenience by staying at those jobs. Having the "security" of a check was not moving me closer to living my life from an authentic place; it was not moving me forward towards a more joyful and meaningful life. No more SOMEDAY stories, no more "should" stories. I decided that my next step was to break the shell, step out, and open my wings and fly high! I was going to listen to my heart and live the life I came here to live because ultimately it was my birthright and my own responsibility, no one else's.

Working on my personal growth has been a continuous process. I have been taking certifications and working with coaches and mentors to achieve my goals and develop my business, Inner Prosperity Academy. I can honestly say that I have zero regrets; it has been a beautiful journey. My life now is very different from how it was before.

How I Define Power

Power means a capacity, an ability we all have inside to do or accomplish something. It's a potential that we all have, a drive that comes from within and ignites a force within you. I would also say that it's an energetic force that is fueled by emotions— both good and not-so-good—like love, joy, desire, purpose, and confidence but also anger, resentment, and guilt. I see power as the unique potential that everyone has to shape her own life. How a person shapes her life depends on the power that she has within to recognize and value her own self-worth.

In my personal life, I've experienced power when I connected with the power I already had within. Basically, I recognized the capacity I have to create and recreate my own life, having the awareness that I shape my own reality. I understood that how much good I was letting into my life was determined by my level of self-worth and that Self-confidence is one of the keys to our Happiness. I understood that the key to boost our self-confidence is to really know ourselves, to see ourselves for who we really are. Some people tend to see themselves through the conditionings that they've gained through life, coming from their families, their culture and the bad experiences that they might have had over the years—I was there myself. But in reality, these only rob us from our feelings of joy and freedom, which are natural to all of us.

When we see ourselves through the distorted lenses of our Conditioned-Self or our ego-mind, and we judge ourselves based on external criteria, we will feel that we don't deserve good things, including how much abundance we let into our lives. We will definitely limit our full potential through this distorted vision, as we don't see ourselves clearly, and we'll let doubt and fear dominate our minds, limiting what we are really capable of achieving.

I realized that having clarity of what is a MUST for me gives me power, joy, and freedom. Then all I had to do was to visualize and take action. Following my inner power in my life has taught me to be responsible and accountable for what occurs in my life. I shifted my mindset and chose not to play the victim role and blame others or external circumstances for my results in life. We all have this same inner power within us; we just have to be aware of it and connect to it. We have to keep in mind that in life we are always creating or recreating, living by design or by default; we don't get to NOT create. If you've been in the victim mindset, if you're living by default, you will let life dictate the terms to you, and ultimately you will create the same results you've been experiencing over and over again.

What Makes a Woman Powerful

The key to connecting to your inner power is based on love— self-love. When you start really loving yourself and being aware of your worth, you will connect with your inner power, which is a conscious choice. By loving and knowing ourselves better, we start being more authentic, more true to ourselves. We then let go of attachments, stop handing over our worthiness to others, and let go of the need to have other people's approval. Ultimately, we must recognize and believe that as spiritual beings here on the planet, we are perfect, whole, lovable, and enough—just as we are.

Since we were born, we have been told by our parents, mentors, teachers, friends at school, and society in general how to act and be. That puts a large amount of pressure on us because we have to measure up to certain "standards" in order to be considered of value. Sometimes, we even base our self-worth on performance, causing ourselves to struggle because our self-worth will be based on those events and their outcomes. It is hard for some people to find their own value and their own power within themselves. People tend to look for things outside of themselves to find or feel that power. This is "Outer Power."

In my opinion, external things like approval from others, having material possessions, and having a good position are all things that do not come from within. They are all based on something that is external to us. This is not real power, but rather a conditioned power. Real power needs to come from *within*. This is why I call it the "Inner Power"—power that doesn't come from external people, causes, or circumstances, but from your own core.

As women, I don't think that we know ourselves well enough because we get distracted by so many external things. Society and the media have a big influence on us. Some of the external things that distract us are: the position that we could have at a given company, how we look, how much money we have, how many good or expensive things we have, our circle of influence, and even approval from people externally, like our parents, our spouse, our friends, or our kids. For a lot of people, everything is external. I'm not saying that I have not been there at some point; I think we have all fallen for these external influences sometimes. It is nice to be financially comfortable and have nice things. Who doesn't like that? But what really matters is what we have within and how we use our own Inner Power to create a life we love and that fulfills us.

Inner Power comes from the connection to your Authentic Self, your true-self, so you're not driven by fear. We live in a fear-based society, which is why everything is conditioned to external things. Your inner power comes from the connection to your Authentic self, when you let yourself be guided by your inner wisdom, when you're kind to yourself (and to others), when your heart can open up and be filled with joy, feelings of gratitude and internal peace, self-love and self-trust, and when you let yourself be curious and creative.

When you live based on Outer Power, you live a life that is not aligned with your Authentic Self and your unique life purpose; you're not really taking the time to connect with yourself and love and value yourself for who you really are. That's why the Inner Power is "the power" that women need to be connected to. We all have that hidden reservoir of limitless sacred energy, waiting, ready, and available for us to connect to it, so we can see miracles unfold in our lives when we are aligned to it.

I believe that a woman is powerful when she unapologetically loves herself first and finds her own voice—when she connects with her Inner Power and her Inner Wisdom, which we all bring to this planet. Because, remember, we're perfect beings. When we shift our mindset and treat that connection as our foundation, I think we are unstoppable and powerful. I also think that when we honor our femininity, and we allow ourselves and others the gift of offering to the world the value of the wisdom hidden within us, WE are powerful, as women. We are the vital and much-needed half of humanity; the other half is men. The world needs our energy so much now with all that's going on. We can leave a great legacy by setting a great example to younger generations.

Tools for Connecting to Your Feminine Power

In order for women to truly connect with their feminine power, they must do some necessary things. I suggest having a daily spiritual ritual. This can mean different things for everybody, but I'll give you a few examples. You might practice meditation every day or practice gratitude. Some people do it in the morning and at night before going to bed. Some people do gratitude journaling, which is great too. Taking a walk and being in contact with nature is a great way to connect with yourself. Some people like yoga, prayer, coloring a mandala, or going to church or their temple. Everyone is different, so we all have to find what works for us.

My personal daily spiritual ritual includes the practice of gratitude every morning. I script, by journaling, how I want my day to go, how I want to feel, etc. I do some meditation. I do Reiki on myself every night before I go to bed. I also like connecting with nature, so I go out for a walk to just appreciate the trees, the birds flying, and the beauty of the flowers (their colors, shapes, etc.), as for me, they're little pieces of art. I also like going to the beach at least once or twice a week and sitting on the sand for a few minutes to meditate, feel the breeze on my skin, listen to the waves, and just be present. All these things help me stay grounded and connected.

When you practice all these things on a daily basis, you will be opening the channels that connect you to your inner voice, your inner wisdom. I wholeheartedly believe that being in alignment with our Authentic Self and our Life Purpose is the way to connect to our Feminine Power. That way we are living from an authentic place. If we don't know our purpose, how can we be authentic? So much anxiety is triggered when we are not aligned to our own truth.

I also believe that when women have low self-esteem, they tend to ignore their needs and take care of others first. By doing this often, women become anxious and burned out. The truth is that we cannot be efficient when we are burned out. When we see ourselves through the lenses of our conditioned self, which is our ego mind, we only see a distorted image or version of ourselves, and that's one of the reasons some of us have self-esteem problems. Our self-love immediately increases when we are aware of our Inner power, when we connect to our Authentic Self and recognize who we really are—how perfect and lovable we are and how wonderful are the things that we have to offer to others.

I don't think it's selfish or narcissistic for us to love ourselves first. Actually, I think it's our foremost responsibility. When we care for ourselves first, we enhance our ability to serve and help others. The airlines' safety instructions advise that in the event of having to use the oxygen masks, parents should put on their own masks before they assist their children. I think it's the same concept. When we care for ourselves first, we enhance our ability to serve and help others. So, the first step in taking loving actions and healing time for yourself is to recognize that you deserve it. When you know your worth, you honor your birthright to feel joyful and happy. Isn't that what we all want, ultimately—to be happy?

To prevent myself from getting lost in work, home, etc., I created an "Unapologetic daily self-care ritual" plan for myself, seeing it as a preventive care plan. By taking care of myself, I prevent a need for many days of down time. I highly recommend my clients to create an "Unapologetic daily self-care ritual," too. It could include meditation, going to the gym, taking walks outside, doing yoga, eating healthy (non-negotiable), reading, coloring a mandala, taking photos, drawing, playing an instrument, being in contact with nature, watching a movie, meeting friends, spending time doing things you love, etc. The idea is to nourish yourself, to nurture yourself, and to do what makes you happy. You owe it to yourself!

Taking time for yourself will also have a positive impact on your relationships because you will be doing what you need to do with a different mindset when you have taken care of yourself first.

Our New Role as Women and Our Challenges

Throughout history, women have been seen as weak and inferior. For many years, we were relegated to the background. Thankfully, times have changed and I think that our new role is based on equality and complementing the other half of humanity—men. Complementing men does not mean imitating, competing, or becoming more like men. I think we are in one of the safest times to fully embrace being a woman. So our role should be based on honoring our femininity and our womanhood, and being of service to the world by offering the value of our beautiful energy and our wisdom, by being authentic, by being true to ourselves, and by expressing our own voices. A very important part of our role is leaving a legacy so that young women can look at us as models of what their dreams and responsibilities can be in this new era. We have so much to offer to complement what the world is missing right now.

Even though the role of women has improved and we're more recognized, some things still are not equal. We still face challenges, even in the most advanced countries. One area would be economic empowerment—there are still salary gaps between what men and women make for the same positions. Even though more and more women have been placed in senior management positions, there are still only a few women holding major public positions. Personally, I would like to see more women participating in political campaigns because I know that would bring fresh insights and a new way of handling politics.

Women are as ambitious, and of course as willing, to be successful as men are, but it's more difficult for women to find a balance between work, love, and family. Women can be judged for wanting a successful career if they have kids. They could be seen as selfish and bad mothers, which puts pressure on them, leading them to limit themselves because they feel guilty. Yet if they stay home with the kids, they could be judged because they're not ambitious enough or successful enough. That doesn't happen to men.

We also can't forget the challenges that some women have to face on a daily basis in other places, like Africa and the

Arab world. Every day, they face violence, discrimination, and suppression. Some women are waking up to the fact that the way they live is not the way it should be; they now know they should be respected equally as human beings. But some other women are still numb; they just see that way of living as part of life. We cannot even begin to imagine what being a woman means living in places like those. It really breaks my heart.

In places where women are being treated poorly, societies are not really functional. I'm not saying that ours is perfect, but we are in a very different—a much better—place, in all senses. We are so blessed to have our lives here. There has been a great advancement, but there's still more to be done—it's a work in progress. By creating awareness and by getting together with other heart-centered women, we can make a difference in other women's lives, women who really need inspiration to take their power back.

We must keep being authentic, having our voices heard, and uniting. We have to work together to improve our role and diminish the challenges that women all over the world are still facing.

From my struggles and pain, I created my own business called *InnerProsperityAcademy.com* to help women live life from an authentic place and find their Life Purpose. With the services and programs that I am offering, I help growth-oriented women who are stuck in an unfulfilling career to recreate their lives, turning them into the ones they came here to live. I want them to feel inspired, to really emerge and shine, and be authentic.

We all come to this planet with a purpose that is as unique as a fingerprint. Finding our Life Purpose is our birthright. It is one of the most courageous things we can do for ourselves and for the world in general because it creates a ripple effect. I have created a unique process, the *Inner Prosperity Process*™, that contains all the necessary interrelated components that are necessary to achieve the life filled with *INNER PROSPERITY, Joy, and Freedom* that we all long for. A prosperous life starts from the inside out, and it creates a ripple effect on other areas of your life. This is the process that I followed myself, and now I'm sharing it with my clients. They are living more balanced and prosperous lives—in all areas.

Now, my own life is different because I went from feeling anxious, unfulfilled, and depressed—living on autopilot—to living from an authentic place with more joy, balance, meaning, clarity, and freedom. I went from working for a paycheck to working for a mission! I'm doing what I really love. I wake up excited and enthusiastic every morning about the day ahead. All I had to do was know that I deserved the life that I wanted to have and give myself permission to want it.

I feel that following my heart and living the life I came here to live has been the most beautiful act of self-love that I've done for myself. Taking those steps in my life is the way that I connected with my feminine power. Being in alignment with who I really am and being able to help others find that for themselves, so they can give their greatness to the world, is the best version of life that I could ever imagine because it creates a ripple effect in the lives of others and the world in general.

CHAPTER 15

Jennifer Bloome

Jennifer Bloome's passion is helping women build and nurture whole life fertility. Through her businesses Anji, Inc. and Fertile Business, she provides mind body spirit tools and coaching to women across the world. She is the creator of the internationally acclaimed meditation series A Journey of the Heart as well as the Magic of Prosperity and Mompreneur Meditations.

Drawing on her background of Psychobiology, Occupational Therapy, Health and Wellness Counseling, Energy Medicine, and Soul Language, she helps women remember how to create from the inside-out. The beautiful part of this is that when creation flows from the inside out, success is in complete alignment with the heart and soul. In addition, there is the exquisite satisfaction of fulfillment and the joyous freedom that comes from giving birth to the life that the soul is longing to express.

Jennifer works with women on all kinds of creations from babies to financial prosperity.

To learn more or connect with Jennifer visit www.JenniferBloome.com.

My Story and My Journey to Power

As a woman, how do you decide who to be? Is there a "best" role (business owner, mother, partner, daughter, employee, etc.) for happiness, joy and success? Whose values and opinions do you listen to in order to decide: society's, your family's, yours? Women are discovering that the specific types of roles they play are less important than knowing who they are at their core and choosing roles that fit this knowledge. We are giving ourselves permission to understand and live from our own innate abilities— our Inner Capital™—while still retaining the essence of how we wish to show up in the world. Knowing this is possible and doing it in your life are two very different skills. My life's journey-to-date has been about discovering and living this shift for myself and creating the opportunity for others to do the same.

My journey to choosing to live from my own innate abilities, or Inner Capital™ as I call it now, began in 1998. After moving to a new state, I'd decided to stay home with my two young children. A part of me easily settled into the exclusive role of "Mom," but another part of me was still not quite satisfied; I wasn't feeling truly fulfilled. And yet, I knew I couldn't go back to the "Employee" role in the way I had before. After being in limbo for quite a number of months, I had a defining moment that changed everything. I was standing in my living room and suddenly, I heard: *There's something more here; there's something you're not seeing. There's a way to be that you're not being.*

I didn't understand exactly what those words meant at the moment; all I knew was something had opened up inside and was pulling me forward. That moment was the start of giving myself permission to look at who *I* wanted to be based on my innate abilities. I realized that up until that point, the path I had been on was really a path of what I thought I *should* be doing, based on expectations and tradition: go to college, get a job, have your family, and work at a job until you retire. And while there's nothing wrong with that path, I gave myself permission to acknowledge that it wasn't working for me.

And so the journey began. Each decision I made—like getting a second advanced degree, taking meditation courses, having my hand analysis completed, or learning my Soul Languages— allowed new gifts and talents to unfold and gave me a better understanding of who I came to BE on this planet. Interestingly, not once during this journey did I know exactly what life was going to look like or my exact destination. I simply followed my intuition. Each time I followed my intuition, I received more and more information about who I was at my core being, which allowed me to make new choices that brought me into alignment with a life path that brought me happiness, joy, and success in many new and different ways.

How I Define Power

As I reflect on the story of my defining moment, I realize that what I was really doing was discovering and tapping into my own power. But what does "power" really mean? The word carries a vast array of connotations that aren't so flattering, especially to us as women. Using your power can sound like you are going to run roughshod over everyone around you, or be the boss who holds a sword over everyone else, or act in a way that is completely outside your values and integrity. This is actually one of the areas I spend a lot of time on with clients—being afraid to be a powerful woman and possibly hurting someone else because of it.

Instead of giving the word those negative connotations, I define power as our fuel as human beings. It's who we are at a soul level. When we are "in our power," we are tapping into our Inner Capital™, that essence of who we are and expressing it. When we take action from this place of power, those actions are taken in integrity with ourselves at a soul level. That is the kind of power that changes the world in a safe, beautiful, and peaceful way.

What Makes a Woman Powerful

In addition to speaking about power in general, we can also talk about Feminine Power. Each of us carries masculine and feminine energies within our beings, and we use both in daily life. As women, we have a natural ability to connect with our feminine energies, our feminine power. I believe at the core of feminine power is the ability to be intuitive, to be intimately connected with the Divine and receive Divine guidance. We are able to deeply listen to ourselves and the Divine and to connect with others in a very authentic way. We are powerful in our ability to listen and get into alignment with the inspired actions that come directly from Source Energy.

The challenge for us women is to know how to connect with our feminine power and not see it as something to be feared or something negative. In society today, action and doing (masculine energy traits) are valued more highly than being still or listening first and then receiving or doing. To use our feminine power, we must be willing to learn to allow quiet in our day-to-day lives—to sometimes step away for a little while from the hustle and bustle of everyday life, and just **be**. Women are innately good at producing and getting things done, but accessing your personal power really does require a time of stillness. We must give ourselves permission to be quiet so that we can start to hear our connection with ourselves, with our soul, and with our own personal power. When we begin to truly understand the power at our core, we are able to feel how acting from this place will only highlight our values, not make us take action in a way that is out of integrity with our values.

Tools for Connecting to Your Feminine Power

Creating a meaningful connection with a higher power or spirit—something or someone beyond ourselves—on a daily basis is one of the many ways that women can tap into and begin to understand and trust their feminine power. One of the ways that I regularly connect is through Nature. For me, being out in Nature grounds me and connects me with Mother Earth. There is an automatic connection with the Divine once you are out with the elements; think of looking at a soaring mountain range, or floating in the ocean or deep lake. In those moments, you can't help but feel connected with that energy that is greater than all of us.

Another way that I connect is by knowing my Soul Languages. Soul Language is a paradigm that provides you a way to understand why you're here on the planet and the personal tools you brought with you for the journey. This paradigm also provides a structure to literally access and communicate with your connection to the Divine—with your Soul. Every morning—and throughout the day—I connect with my Soul via my Soul Languages and receive guidance as well as understand myself in an even more tangible way, which allows me to make new choices in how I live.

For example, one of my Soul Languages (we each have three) is Pioneer. Someone who carries Pioneer as a Soul Language is here on the planet to forge new paths, to think new thoughts. Knowing this about myself solidified my understanding that my path in this lifetime wasn't supposed to be a traditional one. My very essence was asking me to do things differently and be different.

Having a regular practice of connecting with the Divine and your essence is important because women tend to be very busy—we take on multiple roles and we find ourselves tending to others. We are good at filling every moment with action. We end up putting ourselves last, forgetting to take care of our needs or not even knowing enough about ourselves to know what we need. You cannot get to know your own essence when you are spending all your time focusing on others. When I was developing my personal business, the single biggest challenge that I ran into was deciding whether to spend time on myself or on my business or my family. My fear was that if I spent time on myself, or my business, my family would suffer. Of course, I did not want my family to suffer.

I didn't consciously understand how much this dynamic impacted both me and my business until I had spent many years as a business owner. Of course, I knew that family was important to me, but I didn't understand what an impact the value of my family had on my business. For many years, I played really small and didn't allow myself to take steps that would grow my business because I had such an internal conflict about what I thought the results would mean to my family. Once I became conscious of that conflict, I thought deeply about what it meant to me to be a good parent and how that related to growing my business.

I finally came to a place of understanding that in order to be the mother (and woman and business owner) I wanted to be, I had to make myself a priority. If I don't follow what my soul is asking me to do in service to myself and the world around me, I become a pale shade of who I'm really meant to be, and I cannot serve my family well when I'm in that place. Therefore, I worked on creating a business model that honored my family and allowed me to connect with myself. As my children have grown older and more independent, they don't have the same needs as they did before, but it certainly was a journey for me to be able to give myself that permission to honor myself and to nurture myself. Having a sacred practice of connecting to the Divine and to my own feminine power was a crucial part of being able to give myself that permission.

Our New Role as Women and Our Challenges

Certainly I am not the only woman who struggles with how to balance personal needs, family and business. Over the years, the variety of roles open to women has grown significantly—from wife, to mother, to business professionals, to CEOs, to entrepreneurs. These roles continue to grow and change for modern day women. In past decades, the woman's role was to do as many roles as possible. The focus was very much on doing, doing, and doing some more. We were modeling very masculine, action-oriented energy.

As times are changing, I think our new job, regardless of what role we are in, is to model the blend of both feminine and masculine energies. As women acting from our feminine power, we get to model a new way of being in action. First we connect with our feminine power and listen to our intuition, and **then** we take action. We get to be the ones to show how we balance being true to ourselves and providing service to the world.

This is not to say that the transition to our new role is complete. At some level, many of us still have that underlying thought of "Well, I should be able to do everything. I should be able to do what the 1950s women did—take care of everything in the home—and be the modern woman as well, going out into the world and producing."

The way to put the old thinking to rest is to truly know ourselves and know what our greatest gifts are and what we really want. If you're always looking to society to tell you what a woman is supposed to do and be, you're never going to feel comfortable in your own skin or learn to balance all of the roles you play. The more we can truly know ourselves, the more that we can be in balance in our variety of roles. Now we are able to find joy as we live fully within each role.

Inner Capital ™

To lead from who you are as opposed to what others think you should be or do takes great courage. The way to build that courage is to create an intimate understanding of who you are—I call that knowing your Inner Capital™.

Inner Capital™ is the sum accumulation of our wealth of gifts and talents that we came in with as a Soul. This accumulation contains gifts and talents unique to us as individuals, as well as gifts and talents that are ours simply because we are part of the Divine. Examples of our Inner Capital™ include but are not limited to our Soul's mission and purpose, our Soulful personality, our

Divine connection, and our understanding of Universal Truths, including the energy of abundance.

For example, for me Feminine Power is an example of a gift that I possess simply because I am part of the Divine, while Pioneer energy is an individual gift. I am also a mentor and a healer, and I carry the ability to help others get in alignment with the new creations their Souls long to bring into existence. All of these gifts and talents inform the roles I play in day-to-day life and help me choose how I want to express myself in the world. I choose to express all of these in my roles as Wife, Mother, Business Owner, and Daughter.

If I compare these roles to what I played before I became aware of my Inner Capital™, most are the same. However, I come to them from a place of engaging my own power, my own Inner Capital™, which greatly improves my day-to-day joy and happiness as well as my deep sense of fulfillment. When we know and engage our Inner Capital™, I believe that we become powerful beyond measure and that this power comes from a place of integrity and authenticity. Knowing your Inner Capital™ will allow the Universe to bring you joy and prosperity, but it will only happen if you learn to embrace your inner value.

Embracing Your Inner Capital ™

Embracing your Inner Capital™ can be tricky. The very first step, as obvious as it sounds, is to make the decision that you are going to claim your Inner Capital™ as an essential piece of who you are and to use this Capital as a compass to create your life. As women, we are often taught that it is "not nice" or even egotistical to say what we do well. We are supposed to allow others to complement us. But when you remember you Inner

Capital™ is Divinely given, how can claiming it and living from it be ego-driven? Even if you aren't able to articulate fully what your gifts and talents are, I invite you to decide to accept and truly acknowledge that you are a unique individual with unique Inner Capital™. These gifts and talents were intentional when you came in as a Soul; in fact, you chose them in partnership with the Divine.

Finding Your Value

When we **don't** know our Inner Capital™ or accept it or engage it fully, life becomes more of a challenge; it's as if you are literally fighting against yourself. You end up cutting yourself off from the flow of the Divine, which can lead to patterns of lack and not enough. So we end up being without enough time, without enough love, or without enough money. Going one level deeper, you end up living somebody else's idea of who you are or who you're supposed to be. It's a much more painful way to live.

So why don't we all live from our Inner Capital™? There are several different layers to what can keep us from being able to embrace it. I believe that when we come into this body, we fully remember our connection with the Divine—we remember who we are. All you have to do is to look at a little kid playing and simply expressing herself. She is who she is, and she simply lives full out.

Then, our connection to and understanding of our Inner Capital™ begins to be molded by well-intentioned adults in our lives, who teach us about how we "should" be and what we "should" do. For example, let's say you are in school and you do something that helps the teacher. She praises you in front of the class, which of course feels really good. You do something your parent has asked and you get a hug. Then, you do something that you want to do because it feels good to you—like painting all over the dining room table—and you get scolded. This doesn't feel good at all, and part of you makes a choice to never put yourself in a position to be scolded again.

As a result, you start to learn to mold your behavior to what is expected of you; you start to shut off your own internal impulses because you want to make sure you get praised, not scolded. You stop thinking about what you want and instead focus on what someone else believes is right. Essentially, you forget the connection to yourself. So you begin to embrace the layers of other people's beliefs that feel true to you, but they aren't really true in terms of who we are at a Soul level. Your Inner Capital™ then gets covered over by the external beliefs of others.

The deepest layer that blocks our access to our Inner Capital™ is how we perceive our value. So many of us come to believe that it is hard work and achievements and what we produce in the world that determine our value; we believe that our value comes from outside of us. And this can work for us for a while. If there is something more we want, we simply work harder, we "do" more. But there comes a time, a time of crisis—perhaps a health or financial crisis—when you can no longer do what you've always done. Now you begin to question your value and look even more to the outside of yourself to see evidence that you are of value.

The problem with waiting for something external in order to form that validation is this: what you focus on expands. You are in this place of feeling not enough yet because you don't have that external validation to say you're of value, so your dominant belief is now one of "not enough." You receive experiences that match your dominant beliefs, so now you have more experiences happening around you that leave you feeling not enough—like not enough time, not enough money, not enough love. This perpetuates a vicious cycle of waiting for validation but never being able to receive it because we aren't living from our Inner Capital™—because we are waiting for validation from the outside. This is one of the strongest and most insidious blocks to engaging your Inner Capital™.

Tangible Steps

The process of embracing your Inner Capital™, finding your value, and living from who you truly are will be aided by taking a series of steps. First, commit to a daily practice of connecting with the Divine. This daily practice could be listening to an amazing piece of music, getting out into nature, or sitting quietly and journaling. This is important because not only are you directly in connection with Source energy, but you are also, by taking some time for yourself, beginning to recognize the part of **you** that is of the Divine.

A second step to take is to begin to put language to your inner gifts and talents. It only makes sense that the more you know your gifts and talents, the easier it will be to utilize them. We all have a sense of our gifts, but personally I have found it extremely useful to tap into the variety of resources available to share more about your unique signature as a Soul. I've done Hand Analysis, Shamanic Astrology, and Soul Language, just to name few. These kinds of systems can give you insights into your Being that you either couldn't name before or knew about yourself but didn't realize were such gifts. We so often discount ourselves and what we can bring to the world. But the more you can know about your gifts and talents, the more you will be able to connect and embrace your Inner Capital™.

Finally, you need to have a way to release the beliefs you have taken on from other people about who you are and your specific gifts and talents. Some of these old beliefs fall away automatically as you begin to learn more about you. Other times, you need to take a deeper approach to releasing. There are a variety of energy release/energy clearing techniques that work very well; some, you can even do yourself. If you are running into roadblocks, working with a practitioner can be super helpful, as personal beliefs are sometimes hard to see: things seem true because we carry the belief that they ARE true. A practitioner can help you see the old patterns that created the beliefs.

Be gentle with yourself as you begin the process of embracing and living from your Inner Capital™. The more I reflect on my journey, the more I understand that it has really been about knowing, loving, and accepting myself. If we can't love and accept ourselves, life becomes so small and gray. I really encourage every woman reading this book to ask herself, *"What can I let go of or accept about myself that allows an even deeper sense of self-love and self-acceptance?"* Not only will this help allow you to have a life with fewer struggles, but it will also be the most beautiful gift you can give yourself.

CHAPTER 16

Kristina Italic

Transformational Performance Speaker. Author. Occupational Therapist and the Creator of The You Can Do It Diva "Queen Be" Experience where she guides women to unapologetically express their deepest desires, create from their souls and celebrate their ALLness to become QUEEN of their world. She speaks to audiences worldwide about the power of being bold enough to own it, courageous enough to do it and audacious enough to be it, no matter what.

Her "You Can Do It DIVA" movement shows women ways to ROCK their power, share their voice and express their brilliance. Kristina's fiery trailblazing attitude keeps it real and raw and, her sense of vulnerability allows her to touch hearts and change lives forever. Kristina's vision is for ALL women to own every piece of who she is- her grit, her gift and her greatness to live LOUD + LOVELY + LEGENDARY.

She is a #1 Bestselling contributing author in the acclaimed book, Sexy, Fit & Fab Sirens. Kristina will take you on a hip new journey to artfully infuse ALL of who you are - leaving nothing to the side - gracefully integrating your ALLness into becoming the QUEEN BE of your world. To connect with Kristina or learn more visit: www.YouCanDoItDIVA.com.

My Story and My Journey to Power

I AM a #1 Bestselling Author, Speaker, Artist and Leader. I AM a Dreamer. Creator. Believer. I AM a Freedom Junkie. Soul Sister. Community Creator. I AM a Creative Entrepreneur, Visionary, Boundary Pusher, Rebel With A Cause, Sexual and Spiritual Goddess, Badass Beauty and Divine Diva. I AM a Woman On A Mission to impact the world! As I declare who I am to you today, I am taken back to merely a few years ago when I was deeply struggling to know who I was and what I wanted—when I questioned every decision and ultimately my life.

It was New Year's Eve, the last day of what had been the roughest year of my adult life. I had lost everything that year! My relationship had ended with my partner walking out on me and never coming back. I had lost all my money. I had no friends close by—no one I could talk to or any place to go. As I was going to bed the last night of that dreadful year, I had this gut-wrenching ache in my stomach and tears were streaming down my face. I knew in my soul there had to be something more I was supposed to be doing and creating with my life. But I couldn't shake the emptiness and extreme sadness I was feeling. As I lay there reflecting, I knew I would not survive another year like that. I could not have a repeat!

I considered myself a leader who was self-aware and could "make things happen," yet I couldn't figure out how to quiet the dull, draining, and disconnected feeling I had on the inside. I was helping other people live their lives, but I couldn't "fix" my own. I really felt like I was almost too broken to be repaired. And as I was lying there crying myself to sleep, I prayed. I prayed like I never had before. I prayed that if I was supposed to be here on this earth, if I was supposed to be doing something great, if there was a purpose for my life…if I was supposed to have an impact while on this earth, I needed God to let me know. The difference between this prayer and all my other prayers was this: I needed to know so clearly and so loudly that I couldn't drown it out. I needed it to be so bright that I would be blinded by it. I knew on a deep level I was pleading, "Please, God, make it so big that I can't go around it." I knew it had to be so clear and obvious. If not, I was going to miss it. Although I would never have been able to articulate this then, I knew I was so full of sadness, hurt, shame, and guilt that I would have missed God's small signs. I was too shut down and too damaged. I would not have seen, heard, or felt a sign if it weren't blatantly obvious. I had lost all sense of myself that year. I didn't know my wants or my desires. I was so lost and broken that I didn't even know who I really was.

When I woke up New Year's Day, I had an eat-pray-love moment. I felt alive, with the answer to my prayers billboarded on my eyelids. The answers were in the real journey, the inner work I had to embrace from that day forward. Through my journey, I found myself and discovered what made me ME.

My journey to power came from a deep yearning for something more out of my own life and the desire to create something more meaningful, passionate, creative, and expressive. You see, I didn't need to have all the answers or have anything figured out. I just needed to surrender and be open and willing to see the magic and beauty in every moment. When I was able to embrace true openness and willingness, I was divinely guided. My true power came from vulnerability, surrendering, and letting go of all that was familiar. When I embraced the unknown, the uncomfortable, and my uniqueness, creativity and intuition, I was able to grasp my power.

While my journey to power has been a twisty, windy, and an unpredictable road, every experience has made me the woman I am today. For that, I am grateful. I have spent most of my life feeling powerless and ashamed of who I am. To the outside world, I was successful, confident, and the go-to friend, colleague, or partner, but on the inside, I was struggling to know who I was at the depth of my soul. I have turned my journey into the You Can Do It DIVA movement, a platform helping women around the world own their power, share their voice, and express their brilliance. My journey has allowed me to inspire women to live Loud, Lovely and Legendary lives, writing their own rules and speaking their minds with style, attitude, and grace.

Though I clearly, confidently, and articulately share who I am now, getting here has not been without struggles, challenges, darkness, or highs and lows. Through my journey, I've realized life is merely a reel of experiences. We have the amazing gift of experiencing the full spectrum of all life has to give us. We decide if our experiences are good or bad or perhaps opportunities to make us sparkle like the gems we are meant to be. We must never forget that diamonds are created under pressure, only to become radiant and brilliant with sculpting and carving. As you travel through your life, you too may endure intense pressure, sculpting, and carving along the way in order for your true brilliance and clarity to fully shine.

How I Define Power

"Power" has so many meanings to me. Power is our internal boldness, confidence, and fierceness that is unleashed when we are creative, expressive and passionate. Power is being unstoppable or a woman's unwavering essence. Power is a woman's intuition and her ability to connect to herself and the Divine. Power is motivational, influential, and impactful. As a leader, I believe true power is creating other leaders, not more followers. The presence and magnetism a woman exudes when she KNOWS who she is and lives from her soul is pure feminine power. A woman's power comes when she embraces her journey of life and embodies her creativity and self-expression. A powerful woman is not afraid of ROCKING her life as she sees fit, in a way that is truly her own and perhaps loud, wild and unruly.

A woman walking into a room confidently, boldly exuding authority and presence without reservation, owning her every step and knowing exactly who she is—that is power. She is not seeking mere attention or approval, but rather captivating attention. She embodies her feminine essence, expressing herself fully and embracing her body wholly. Like moths, others are drawn to her light—she shines.

What Makes a Woman Powerful

A woman's power is not forced or declared, but rather felt and experienced through her presence, captivating essence, and magnetic energy. She knows what she has to offer and is so confidently grounded in who she is; her light is irrefutable. She is powerful because she owns who she is innately, FLAWS and all.

She embraces her full expression in every moment and lets go of perfection. Power is living artfully from your soul.

When a woman has the courage to share her dreams, can commit to stepping into the unfamiliar, and is bold enough to "figure it out" as she goes, she is powerful. A woman is powerful when she is living fully present, rocking her confidence and standing boldly in her femininity. I believe women are unstoppable in whatever they decide to do! Women are powerful when they break the rules and beliefs that keep them from their true potential and unleash fierceness, allowing them to soar to unreachable heights. A woman is powerful, too, when she is comfortable in her vulnerability. When she is not afraid to expose her mess, her rawness or her grit, and stretch beyond her comfort zone, she is powerful.

Discernment and mastery of her own uniqueness gives a woman the ability to lead from a place of love, compassion, and integrity; standing fearlessly on her purpose gives a woman power. Having relentless determination to pursue what matters most to her amidst being uncomfortable and unfamiliar with what lies ahead unlocks a woman's power. A woman's ability to multitask and collaborate—knowing that true greatness only comes when she unites with others—demonstrates her power. When she leads from a place of love and compassion to serve and impact the lives of others, her power shines. A woman is powerful when she is able to confidently look outside herself and find a tribe of women supporting one another's dreams, uniqueness, and creativity, cultivating opportunity and possibility. Such like-minded and like-hearted women ALL will rise together. ALL will become stronger. ALL will create greater impact in their lives, community, and the world around them. A woman is powerful when she knows WHO she is and that she can become WHOMEVER she wants to be and create WHATEVER she desires.

Tools for Connecting to Your Feminine Power

One of my favorite ways to help women connect with their feminine power is through creative self-expression. Creating space in your schedule for fun, play, and pleasure is essential to connecting with your creativity, self-expression, and intuition. A quick and simple way to reconnect is by closing your eyes and asking yourself, "What do I want?" Give yourself time to feel the answer in your body without judgment. Another way to reconnect with your intuition is by making the commitment to yourself that before answering or obligating yourself to anything, you will breathe and check in with yourself before responding. Giving yourself permission to check in before answering begins creating internal trust, therefore allowing your body and intuition to guide you. The more you allow your intuition to guide you and tune inward, the more you rebuild the trust within. When you have internal trust with your body, intuition, and the Divine, decision making becomes easier, you will feel more aligned within, and your awareness and discernment will become heightened.

Nurture yourself. If you want to connect with your feminine power, start by making YOU a priority. Get out in nature. Get out of your head and into our body. Move.

Movement, in my opinion is one of the best ways to reconnect with your feminine power. Personally, dance is my favorite way to let go and move. When you move to the rhythm of a beat, you allow your body to feel the vibration and feel what she wants to do instead of making anything happen. Dancing forces you to be in pure flow of allowing and receiving. Feminine power is fluid and flowing, which in essence is the art of allowing. It is exactly what movement and dancing allow you to do—feel the beat or rhythm and then express through your body, or receive and then allow. When you move, you release stagnant energy into flowing energy. Without this release or energy flow throughout your body, you may experience tension, stiffness, pain, discomfort, anxiety, worry, self-sabotage, doubt, fear, judgment, and many other aliments, illnesses, diseases, and non-virtuous feelings. So, turn up that music and get dancing!

If you are feeling stuck or overwhelmed and need to reconnect with your intuition, self-expression and feminine essence, STOP whatever you are doing and MOVE. Take a hike, do a yoga class, walk, or try something new. It doesn't really matter as long as you: Stop. Breathe. Move. Get out of your head and into your body.

Your inner child is a creative being—let her out to play and have some fun. Somewhere along your way, you may have forgotten what it's like to be free and creative. So one of my favorite tips to unleash your feminine power and creativity is through play and expression. Allow yourself permission to play. Try something you've never tried before, or incorporate something you love into your life again. Maybe it's dancing, painting, listening to music, baking, drawing, reading books, sitting by the ocean, sailing, sewing, or perhaps woodworking. Maybe your personal flavor is going to the theater or a fashion show. GO. There is no time like the present. Nix the excuses and GO. Find a show and GO. If you are still feeling stuck, try going into a really fun and flirty art gallery—another one of my personal favorites. Just go! Do something that will inspire you, feed your spirit, and make you feel like a child again. It is so important to allow yourself to do things that make you happy because if you don't know what makes you happy, nobody else can either. And if you don't know what that is…STOP right now and ask yourself, "What makes me happy?" It may not come right away, and that is perfectly okay. If you are really stuck and don't have a clue, just start trying things out. Trust me, it won't be long before you figure out what you don't like, and then you can go from there. It's a process—so have fun with it! No judgment. Just play.

Give yourself permission to explore, create, fail, be messy, imperfect, and do it ALL over again. Believe me, life is way more fun this way.

All too often women isolate themselves, turning their focus and attention to everyone else and taking the scraps of whatever is left over for themselves. Women are natural collaborators and gatherers and have so many responsibilities that the idea of asking for help is still looked upon as failure. This has got to STOP! It is DESTROYING women.

I am no different than any other woman. I, too, have found myself lost in my work, relationships, and roles, repeatedly shoving my own wants, needs, and desires aside. I lost myself so deeply that I no longer recognized my own voice or knew who I was, and I questioned if my life was even worth living. I have experienced firsthand the effects of not making myself a priority or honoring my commitments to myself or my wants, needs, and desires.

I find it fascinating that most men will always put their needs first. I used to be frustrated by it, but then I realized that it's an amazing quality. They will always put the oxygen mask on first before anyone else because they know with every fiber of their beings that if they don't, they won't survive. And if they don't survive, neither will anyone else. This, too, is true for women. We know this intellectually, but somewhere along the way we accrued an internal conflict embedded with guilt and shame around tending to ourselves or making ourselves a priority. This shoves us deeper into isolation, quieting our voices, dismissing our power, and limiting our true expression.

Women have a voice and are able to create the life they desire. We as women need sacred relationships with other women that are supportive, encouraging, connected, loving, and compassionate—allowing us to fully express our creativity, our femininity, our uniqueness, and our innate brilliance.

Women need a sisterhood that is a safe sanctuary where they can fully express themselves. A sisterhood that does not tear down, but rather builds up. It is a space where women can come together without judgment or fear-based interactions. A powerful sisterhood cultivates and nurtures growth, greatness, creativity, self-expression, collaboration, and possibility. A sisterhood allows women to come together, raising our vibration collectively in the world.

By not honoring our commitments to ourselves, we are subconsciously and energetically saying to the world, "Please don't honor me or your commitments to me. I'm not worth it. I don't even honor my own needs." As women, we must take time for ourselves and value the importance of this commitment to our souls. Too many women are not giving themselves permission to attend to their own basic self-care needs. This is not ok! If you want to be powerful, if you want to be fully alive, expressive, the best version of yourself, and embodying your true essence—you MUST take care and nurture yourself. You cannot be the best version of yourself—the best woman, the best wife, mother, daughter, sister, business woman, community leader, change maker, or influencer—if you're not taking responsibility for yourself, your actions, your values, your wants, your needs, and your desires. You have to honor all of YOU before anyone else can.

CELEBRATE YOU! Have "me dates" or "artist dates" to stay inspired, creative and soulful. Turn the music up and dance. Strut around in stilettos and skivvies—try it. Its fun! Have jam sessions at every stoplight simply because you can. Start doing WHATEVER makes you feel ALIVE. Remind yourself daily, "I have a name, a unique essence, and an identity that does not involve anyone other than who I AM."

Every woman is uniquely gifted and powerful. Every woman deserves to be the QUEEN of her own life. Every woman must take responsibility for herself and nurture her creativity, her expression, her voice, her feminine power—her art. When a woman lives from her soul, she is fully alive, expressed, and radiant, and her essence exudes creativity, playfulness, and passion. She is art. She is powerful.

My last oh-so-valuable tip I think you will love is…invest in yourself. If you want to go after your dream and bring your vision to life, or if you are feeling stuck or in transition, or if you are itching to accelerate the process into greater leadership and power, INVEST in YOU. No one has all the answers—hire a coach or mentor to support you along the way. Each of us only knows what we know, and we can't see all of our blind spots. No one gets to the Olympics without investing in herself, committing to her vision, and finding the perfect coach who sees her brilliance and is willing to push her boundaries. A coach will mirror what you need and guide you to where you need to go. A good mentor or coach will see your innate brilliance, elicit your unique creative expression, and push you out of your comfort zone, so you too will experience the queen you are meant to be—fully rocking your FABULOUSNESS, of course.

Our New Role as Women and Our Challenges

Entrepreneurship and small businesses will change the world. Women are starting nearly 1,300 new businesses every day, which is 68% more than just one year ago. Women are creating momentum and movement in how business is being done around the world. We are leading our lives from our souls, our artistry, our passion, and our purpose. We are changing the world for all humanity and creating new opportunities, new visions, and new ideas. We are integrating our dreams, purpose, leadership, and art.

We are infusing our innate gifts of play, creativity, imagination, and femininity into the linear structure of traditional business, which is masculine driven and outcome based. Women are creating businesses from their heart and soul, capitalizing on their uniqueness and facilitating a massive shift in our masculine-skewed system. We are paving a new, multidimensional, and feminine approach to business, allowing our gifts, talents, creativity, and power to shine in a formerly linear system, thus shifting the business paradigm back to a more balanced spectrum.

I see the new role of women as being that of creative entrepreneurs—creating from their soul and uniting their purpose, leadership, and art into business. In these new roles, women will carry on as the leaders of our communities, leaders of our businesses, and leaders of change around the world.

The Dalai Lama said, *"The western woman will save the world."* I couldn't agree more. This gets me so excited! It is a great time to be alive in the world as a woman. It is the perfect time to be a woman. Women are changing the world—but, only if we share our voice.

It is happening. I promise! I see it every day. Women are sharing their voices now more than ever before. They are expressing their creativity, uniting and supporting one another, and creating change. New opportunities open up every day, allowing women to share their gifts, their brilliance, and their artistry with the world.

Women have figured out that we can have our cake and eat it too. Thank goodness! It is so much more fun this way. Who doesn't want to have their cake and eat it too? Women are ambitious, driven, strong, and powerful. We no longer have to define our success or sense of being through a masculine definition of what it means to be a woman or successful. We are rising together and shedding the masculine masks that have kept us shoved in a box. We are tired of being shamed and shh'd! We are taking a stand and saying, "Thank you for this opportunity, but no thanks. I am going to do it MY way, the feminine, creative, and intuitive way." We are playing to our strengths instead of being shamed or dismissed by being told, "You're too emotional," "You can't let your emotions get the best of you," or "If you want to get to the top, you'd better think like a man." Not anymore! This is the old paradigm by which women were told to abide in life and business. We are now playing by our rules, and there have been some major changes. Now more than ever, woman are pursuing their dreams, running businesses, sharing their artistry, expressing their creativity, having families, and LIVING from their SOULS.

Women have taken what has worked from the old paradigm and have used the momentum and pendulum swing of business as an opportunity to flourish and run with it. Women are starting new businesses like never before—working on-the-go, creating flexibility, and making time to be with their families or go on vacation. With the Internet, micro-businesses, small businesses, and network marketing, just to name a few, the possibilities are endless. We are conducting business by our own rules and on our own terms.

We are taking a stand and breaking the rules of how business and life are "supposed" to be done. We are asking and searching for other women to help us and join our team. We are finding our sisterhood. We are asking questions and figuring things out together, making the unknowns a lot less scary. We are SHINING and being noticed in the marketplace! This is true feminine leadership with collaboration. Competition is old school. Collaboration is allowing women to work smarter with more freedom and FUN, totally ROCKING their lives.

I believe that as creative entrepreneurs woman are now creating businesses not just to accrue revenue, but to lead from their souls to create positive change in the world while giving back to their communities and paying it forward to others. Women are collaborating and creating sisterhoods in unity, serving more and receiving more. Gone are the days when women went into the office having to "Think Like A Man" in order to climb the career ladder. We are THINKING like WOMEN and ACTING like WOMEN.

One challenge we may face, however, is that as business and life move more into a woman's home and toward an on-the-go lifestyle, she may have a slippery slope into isolation and loneliness. The modern woman has to purposefully and intentionally commit to her overall well-being and self-care. As her demands intensify and her roles become continually intertwined, it could become even harder for her to prioritize herself and her needs. The modern woman will experience more flexibility, freedom and space to create if she is able to value her own voice and prioritize her well-being.

When women are working outside the home, they interact with more people on a daily basis and work, in turn, becomes a social experience of sharing and connecting. Women are more apt to meet up for a coffee or lunch during a break from work or a cocktail or dinner after work. However, with the paradigm shift of business into our homes out of the office and corporations, a woman will have to consciously and deliberately find ways to connect, create, and collaborate with other like-minded and like-hearted women.

Another challenge I feel could arise for the modern woman is being able to let go and be free of judgment, guilt or shame as the paradigm shift swings into full effect and the demands on her intensify. I feel this could be a constant internal battle. Allowing herself to be in the unfamiliar, unknown, and the uncomfortable, and at times operate fully from this place, requires her to surrender, trust, and allow the Divine to take the reins and guide her. Three of the most powerful and effective tools a woman can use are trust, surrender and allowing, but these can also be the most difficult to implement and practice. When things are unpredictable, unknown, and uncertain, modern women are forced to completely step out of their comfort zones and lean into their edges. Instead of resisting and intensifying their struggles, they need to trust the process and surrender. Doing this isn't a science; it is art.

Your life is your work of art. Your dreams are priceless. Your talents, gifts, and unique artistry were given ONLY to you. How will you express your ART to the world?

CHAPTER 17

Alice Ukoko

 Alice Ukoko has dedicated her life to raising the profile of African Women globally, driven by her belief that African women need to be recognised as important stakeholders who play a pivotal role in the survival of Africa and in turn the world. She disagrees with the victim construct and negative international portrayal of women and Africa. This negative imaging of African women must change in order to end the growing abuse and violence faced by African woman and girls not just in Africa, but across the world.

Alice's international campaigning ended direct military dictatorship in Nigeria in 1999 and her humanitarian dedication to women and humanity has earned her worldwide recognition. In 2007 she attempted to contest the governorship of Delta State of Nigeria to directly change the political landscape.

Alice believes that women have Divine Authority to bring balance to the world and to heal Africa of its negative past and backwardness. Alice was recently appointed the Regional Director for West Africa to establish the necessary administrative structure to bridge existing gaps between governments and civil society Africa. Establishing the women's commission in Cote d'Ivoire represents a major milestone in achieving gender equalization, democracy sustainable peace and development of Africa. Learn more at www.womenofafrika.org.

A Special Message from Alice Ukoko, Founder of Women of Africa

When Vanessa contacted me to discuss making Women of Africa the recipient of the proceeds of this wonderful book and invited me to share my story, I recognized that a special gift was being given to me—the gift of sharing my lifelong work with a wider audience. For this, I am eternally grateful.

I am driven by my passion to serve and have become a speaker who inspires others, but until now, I found it difficult to sit down and talk about myself. I am an African woman who grew up in Africa and the United Kingdom, one whose life experiences are shared by many women. I married into an abusive relationship in the UK at a time when domestic violence was seen as a private affair. Without support, I found myself trying to survive challenges that were an extension of my childhood of enslavement. I used the legal system, which was helpful to some extent, but in the end, I found that what kept me going was my determination to survive for myself and my children.

There were times that I felt that life was not worth living, but as a mother I felt that I had a duty to stay alive so that my children could survive and do well in their own lives. To stay focused and sane through those days, I enrolled in a part-time degree law course with the London University. This stretched me greatly, as it meant I worked during the week while supporting my children through their own education and then attended classes on Saturdays. I remember sleeping through some of my lectures. As an African woman, hard work is my middle name, though, so I found ways of learning and understanding my courses so well that I became one of the best students during my time there—as I was later told by the college authority with a handshake. Indeed, I completed the five-year part-time program in two and a half years (Sept. 1989 to July 1992). I gained a Bachelor of Laws Degree LLB (Hon. London).

I have lived my life for others, including my children, and I feel an amazing sense of responsibility for my family, my community, and the world to the point that I feel their pain. I feel that what I do from day to day is controlled and propelled by an unseen force, and my drive in life is to keep the world safe.

In August 2014, I felt a strong urge to document my thoughts on specific issues, so that when I am no longer alive in this lifetime, my thoughts and my words would continue to speak to the world. My first recorded interview on YouTube summarized my work in broad terms. I was able to talk about the African Women's Congress and the creation of a women's commission representing an international institution that bridges the gap between governments and civil society Africa. I also seized the opportunity to talk about my spirituality and guiding philosophy. This was the first time I was able to talk openly about matters of spirituality that are so important to me. With the creation of the women's commission, I feel my work here has been accomplished.

It has been my responsibility to always speak my truth. I also acknowledge that whether or not the world hears me is not my responsibility. We must all speak our truths, regardless of the outcome.

In 2014, my health started to break down and I was hospitalized for three weeks so that medical staff could trace the origin of my emerging health challenges. Various tests, including explorative keyhole surgery, confirmed that I had cancer of the lining of my abdomen, an aggressive type of cancer.

I have a very positive mental attitude towards life, which has helped me meet the challenging task of fighting this disease. I am strong, although I admit there are times when I am not able to leave my bed and I am weak on my feet. I continue to do my work, which amazes people, but it is what drives me and why I am here.

My heart is connected to the Divine in us all, so I am aware of the continuing challenges facing women and all humanity. About three weeks into my chemotherapy treatment, my attention was drawn to the plight of grassroots women across Africa. These women continue to engage in economic and social activities for their families and their communities, but without any support. To address this issue, Women of Africa is creating and launching African Women's Economic and Social Fund to support women through a small revolving credit program and seed money. These funds will be available to groups and women who do not have access to any form of financial support. I am confident that through this project, Women of Africa will be able to contribute to the eradication of hunger in Africa.

My quest to achieve international recognition for African women is yielding positive results. The UN Women recognized the work of Women of Africa in a letter dated November 10, 2014 and requested that WOA apply for Consultative Status with the UN NGO Branch and UN Agencies globally. This is a major achievement, as it opens doors for women to sit around policy decision-making tables with governments. There can be no sustainable development anywhere in the world until women take their rightful place alongside others in policy decision making.

As a result of this success, the Chair of Women of Africa, Anne Crossfield, has taken our crusade to the European Parliament and Commission. I am looking forward to the recognition of the EU, as I know this will open many more doors across the world for WOA.

In October 2014, the Women's Regional Director for West Africa was appointed to work with us to establish the first office of the Commission in Cote d'Ivoire. I am hopeful that the creation of the regional office to coordinate the planting of offices in sixteen West African countries will further the engagement of women in Africa's recovery.

Although I am undergoing chemotherapy, I continue to work to ensure that even if I am approaching the end of my present lifetime, I am able to leave knowing I have created more ease for the women who will continue with this work once I have gone.

No one can predict the future; however, the result of my treatment thus far points to my full recovery, bringing to realization my healing and freedom from cancer.

I am deeply grateful to the Divine within us all and to the pure love of my children, friends and colleagues, who have helped me face this disease and allowed me to look forward to my healing and future. I am deeply grateful, too, to Vanessa for creating this wonderful book that will touch so many women across the world.

Acknowledgement

As with any book project, there are many people involved in the manifestation of this labor of love and whom I'm incredibly grateful for.

The first person I need to thank is Gina Cloud. The minute she heard about The Power of Being a Woman book project she approached me and offered to help in any way possible. She saw the vision of the book and helped me to stay true to it throughout this entire process.

I'd like to thank Tanya Egan Gibson for editing this book so brilliantly and Julie Csizmadia for making the book come to life by designing the book layout.

Thank you to all the contributing ladies in this book for believing in the vision and mission of this project and for sharing their stories here so that other women can follow in their footsteps. I'm truly inspired by all of you!

A special thank you goes out to Katie Day for introducing me to Alice Ukoko from Women of Africa, who became the beneficiary of the book. It was very important for me that this book carried a deeper meaning behind it and offering it as a gift to a beautiful and powerful non-profit that helps women empower themselves seemed like the perfect fit.

On a more personal level, I would like to thank my entire family for supporting and believing in me, specially my husband Bassam Halloum whose love and encouragement always inspires me to be the best that I can be.

Last, but most definitely not least, I need to thank the Divinen Mother for inspiring me to create a project like this and for giving me the courage to keep going, even when things got a little challenging.

~ *Vanessa Halloum*

CPSIA information can be obtained at www.ICGtesting.com
Printed in the USA
BVOW10s1249180715

408911BV00024B/123/P